Making Great Decisions

Workbook

Making Great Decisions

Workbook

For a Life Without Limits

T.D. Jakes

ATRIA PAPERBACK

New York   London   Toronto   Sydney

ATRIA PAPERBACK

A Division of Simon & Schuster, Inc.
1230 Avenue of the Americas
New York, NY 10020

First Atria Paperback edition June 2009

ATRIA PAPERBACK and colophon are trademarks of Simon & Schuster, Inc.

For information about special discounts for bulk purchases,
please contact Simon & Schuster Special Sales at
1-800-456-6798 or business@simonandschuster.com.

The Simon & Schuster Speakers Bureau can bring authors to your live event. For
more information or to book an event, contact the Simon & Schuster Speakers Bureau
at 1-866-248-3049 or visit our website at www.simonspeakers.com.

Manufactured in the United States of America

10 9 8 7 6 5 4 3 2 1

ISBN: 978-1-4165-4752-5

contents

Introduction
Before You Decide

A workbook helps you step out of the book (words) and go into action. This workbook is designed to bring the ideas and information you read in *Before You Do* to life. Through journaling, self-talking, and other interactive exercises, you will be equipped to contemplate, plan, and act. Think of the three words in the book title as the game plan for this workbook.

"Before" is the opening section of each chapter—**questions for contemplation.** I ask you to take a journal or piece of paper and pen to a quiet place. First, sit down, close your eyes for a minute, take a few deep breaths to get centered, and then spend at least five minutes (longer if you can) simply to contemplate the list of questions provided on that chapter's specific topic.

Then your task is to write out your answers. This writing down is separate from the contemplation. It's the **"You"** section in each chapter. Writing down the thoughts that surface as you contemplate is to help you get to know yourself and accept yourself for who you are. The process will be most effective if you think first, then write. It's two separate steps. It's all about you. Be as honest as possible. No one but you will read what you write. The more truthful you can be, the more helpful the answers will be to you as you make decisions. And, periodically, when the issues you write about arise in your life, you can refer back to your notes and the corresponding chapters for support. I'll ask you to read, reread, and think about the answers you've written. It's part of the process of "doing you"—getting to know yourself and accepting your style of decision making.

Finally, each chapter ends with a **"Do"** section, where you step out of the book, the words, and make a plan of action. This section includes exercises, checklists, and other activities to help you bring the ideas of the chapters to life. Have fun with this section, be creative; think of it less like exercises and more like ideas and suggestions for making sure the decisions you make in your life, especially the relationship decisions, are the best they can be, before you do.

Making Great Decisions

Workbook

one

Reflect, Discern, Decide
The Process of Making Good Decisions

Before you begin this portion of the Making Great Decisions Workbook, *read Chapter One, "Before You Take the First Step—Reflect, Discern" (pages 13–29), in* Making Great Decisions *(formerly titled* Before You Do*).*

Good decision making in relationships, business, or anything results from a process of reflection–discernment–decision. Sound decisions are based on great information, so the more significant the question, the more due diligence is required to make the correct decision. Important decisions demand stewardship. If we are to be good stewards of great opportunities, we must show respect for those opportunities by the level of diligence at which we prepare for the next move.

"Before" (Questions for Contemplation)

We each have our own style and ways to approach the decision-making process. Some of us tend to know exactly what we want. We make up our minds quickly and act immediately. Others prefer to deliberate for a long time, weighing all the angles and options before deciding what to do. It is important to know your decision-making style so that when you have to make one, you will know exactly what you need to do to make sure your decision is the best one for you and those around you.

Find a quiet place that isn't crowded and sit down. Go for a walk in a beautiful park and find a bench under a wonderful tree or set up a chair in your yard or on your porch. If you live in an urban area go to a quiet local coffee shop or diner. If you can't go outside, find a private, comfortable place in your home or apartment where you won't be disturbed. Sit down, close your eyes for a minute, take a few deep breaths to get centered and then just spend at least five minutes (longer if you can) simply contemplating the following questions:

1. How do you usually go about making decisions in your life? Are you prone to make up your mind quickly and act immediately? Or are you someone who deliberates for a long time, weighing all the angles, before you make a decision?

2. How often do you typically change your mind once you've made a decision? How often do you second-guess yourself regarding a decision you've made?

3. Which is easier for you—to make a small daily decision (what to wear, what to order at dinner, etc.) or to make a larger decision with greater consequences (a major purchase, a committed relationship, etc.)?

4. How often do you let others make decisions for you? When have you chosen to make no decision and allow circumstances to dictate your direction for you?

5. Most of us have some regrets. Consider your life. What decisions do you regret the most? Why?

"You" _____

Now that you have thought about the questions, honestly write out your answers below.

I usually go about making decisions in my life by . . .

_____

_____

_____

_____

The decisions I regret the most are . . .

_____

_____

_____

_____

Why?

_____

_____

_____

_____

If your answers flowed easily, skip the next list of questions and go directly to **"What does it mean?"** on page 5. If you're staring at those blank lines, you might want to get your mind flowing by considering the following statements, using one of the choices below:

Almost always   Occasionally/Infrequently

Usually/Frequently   Rarely/Almost never

I am prone to make up my mind quickly.

I am prone to act immediately.

I am someone who deliberates for a long time before I make a decision.

I am someone who weighs all the angles before I make a decision.

I change my mind once I've made a decision.

I second-guess myself regarding a decision I've made.

It's easy for me to make a small daily decision (what to wear, what to order at dinner, etc.).

It's easy for me to make a larger decisions with greater consequences (a major purchase, a committed relationship, etc.).

I let others make decisions for me.

I have chosen to make no decision.

I allow circumstances to dictate my direction for me.

I have regrets.

Turn over your paper or put the book aside and again, just sit quietly. Close your eyes or gaze at something beautiful—the clouds in the sky, a photo of a loved one, a fountain, the steam coming off your coffee cup, or a vase of flowers. Spend at least another five minutes just thinking about what you've written, letting it sink in.

Looking at your answers to the individual statements, go back and write your answers to the questions at the top of this section.

What does it mean?

This exercise is designed to help you gather information you can use going forward as we proceed through this book and as you live your life. It is not intended to condemn you or get you to punish yourself for anything you've done. Until we understand the mistakes of our past, we simply continue to repeat them. It is important to make peace with our decisions and any regrets by taking ownership of what we did, apologize where necessary, and then work to move forward. Dr. Maya Angelou said something very profound about looking back over our mistakes: "When you know better, you do better."

One of the reasons we make ill-informed decisions is because we aren't sure who we are as a person. This is not to say that we aren't a good and decent person. But when you haven't decided who you want to be in the world, what you stand for, what you consider right and wrong, what you like, and what you dislike, then when faced with situations where you need to make decisions, you may be easily swayed by the wants, needs, desires, and opinions of others.

Now read over your answers again. Do you see patterns emerging? Are there things that you wrote that invoke a strong reaction, positive or negative? Circle them. These are priceless clues to how you've made decisions in the past, and can perhaps show a pattern in how you view situations as well as give you ideas about what you can do in the future to avoid the same scenarios.

Knowing who you are and what you want is vital to participating in a successful relationship. While it seems counterintuitive to focus on who you are versus on who the two of you are as a couple, the whole is only as strong as the parts. Truly successful and mutually beneficial relationships are based on each party being truthful and upfront about their real wants, desires, and feelings. While certainly as a couple, you must make decisions together, decisions about who you are as a person and what you want your life to be are yours alone to make. Allowing someone else—a relationship partner, a friend, a parent, or anyone else—to make decisions for you is a mistake. When you let someone else decide who you are and what you want, you give away the power that God gave to you.

Your true values

This next exercise will help you clarify your true values. In the column on the left, make a list of the five things you value most, the things that are most important to you: for example, being a good partner, being a reliable friend, keeping your word, always telling the truth, being an excellent teacher, doctor, or father—whatever it is that you value most. Then, in the column on the right, describe what that means to you. Say you want to be a good friend. Does that mean always telling the truth? Always being there to lend an ear or support?

1. _____   _____

2. _____   _____

3. _____   _____

4. _____   _____

5. _____   _____

Rate yourself, and those to whom you relate, on each of
your five true values

Think about how you spend the majority of your time. Do you practice or
exhibit these values?

Almost always   Occasionally/Infrequently

Usually/Frequently   Rarely/Almost never

Value   How I practice/exhibit this value

_____   _____

_____   _____

_____   _____

_____   _____

_____   _____

Now make the same rating for those you spend the most time with.

Value   How he or she practices/exhibits
                                         this value

_____   _____

_____   _____

_____   _____

_____   _____

_____   _____

Is what the lists reveal in keeping with who you say you want to be? If there is a gap, ask yourself what you need to do to bring yourself and those you relate to into closer alignment with what you truly value.

Now write out your five values—for example, honesty, integrity, a knowledge seeker, intimate relationships—on an index card and tape it to your bathroom mirror, to your computer at work, put it in your wallet, someplace where you will see it each day. Let it absorb into your consciousness; it is already what you believe inside of you. By seeing it each day it will begin to move from your inner recesses to your everyday thoughts. Then when decisions arise, small or large, ask yourself, "Is what I am about to do or say in keeping with who I am as a person?"

"Do"

I know who I am and I know those I relate to, but how do I decide what I want? Make a list of pros (reasons to make the decision, things that are good about it) and cons (reasons not to make the decision, things that could be bad). Literally write out both sides of the issue and see which side of the list is longer. It seems simple, but it works!

The decision I have to make is . . .

_____

Pros   Cons

_____   _____

_____   _____

----------   ----------

----------   ----------

----------   ----------

----------   ----------

----------   ----------

----------   ----------

----------   ----------

Judge each item on each list against your five true values. If an item is in keeping with one of your true values, circle it. The list that has the most items circled indicates the direction of your decision if you are being true to you.

Working out the big three decision killers—procrastination, mind-change, regret

Procrastination

Do you procrastinate? Let me caution you. As Dr. Phil often says, "There is no trying. You are either doing or not doing." And if you are doing nothing you are not making a decision. Sitting back and pretending not to see a situation for what it is or procrastinating about what to do until something happens where you have no choice but to go one way or another is just as bad as letting others make decisions for you. It's passive and, in the end, won't be likely to serve you very well. Sometimes circumstances are what they are, but you always have the choice to decide who you want to be within them.

What are the reasons you cannot make a decision?

Reasons I can't make a decision   Eventual decider

_____   _____

_____   _____

_____   _____

_____   _____

_____   _____

For each item on your list, note how the decision will be made if you do nothing. For example, another person, legal system, etc.

Now write one reason you *can* make the decision:

_____

Changing your mind

Changing your mind frequently once you've decided to do something could be a sign that you are not taking an *adequate amount of time* to consider all of your options or the ramifications of your decisions before you make them. If you find yourself second-guessing yourself regarding a decision you've made, remember that feeling of angst and uncertainty the next time you have a decision to make and think twice, weighing all of your options, before proceeding ahead.

Review your pro and con list above and your overlay of your five values *before* you decide. If you have an urge to change your mind, look carefully at your list and reaffirm that your decision reflects your values.

Strong reactions, regrets

Strong feelings of sadness or anger are a sign that you are not at peace with some decision you've made and that you may regret it. Go back to your five true values. Are they really your true values? Only you can answer. Perhaps you would like honesty, integrity, knowledge seeking, and intimate relationships to be what you value most, but in reality, what you value is status, being accepted by your peers, material prosperity, and hassle-free relationships. Be honest. If you have decided based on who you are, you may have bittersweet feelings, even feelings of loss or sacrifice, but probably not hollow regret.

Let go of regrets

There are a number of ways you can let go of regrets.

Pray

In your own words. Or if you need some help try this simple prayer:

Dear God, please forgive me for _____. I understand that I hurt

_____ and myself and for that I am sorry. From this experience, I have learned

_____ and_____ and_____.

I ask that you support me through this situation and help me to forgive others as well

as myself for my part. Now that I have more understanding, please help me to move

forward into the future and to do better when faced with a similar situation next

time. Amen.

Ask yourself what you would do differently if you could go back in time. Would you call to say you are sorry? Write a letter?

Write a letter

Writing letters to those who have hurt us or to those we have hurt can be a very therapeutic experience. Even if you never send it, the intent can be just as genuine.

Your approach to making decisions, your true values, and insight into the big three decision killers are the first steps of reflection and self-discernment. But the next issue is almost as important.

two
Going from Blame to Aim
Finding Solutions to Relationship Challenges

> *Before you begin this portion of the* Making Great Decisions Workbook, *read Chapter Two, "Before You Blame—Accept Responsibility" (pages 31–46), in* Making Great Decisions *(formerly titled* Before You Do).

B lame prevents you from making good relational decisions because you must, at least, own your issues and take responsibility for their resolve, if not for their origin. As with so many problems in our lives, maybe you didn't cause this particular one, but it has fallen to your lot to fix it, rather than place blame.

"Before" (Questions for Contemplation)

Use the same process as in Chapter One. Start in a quiet, comfortable place where you can think. Get centered and then just spend at least five minutes (longer if you can) simply contemplating the following questions. Remember, be as honest as possible with yourself. The more honest you are the more growth and change you will experience.

1. Do you tend to take too much responsibility for others (such as your children) or not enough? What impact has your attitude had on family members and others around you?

2. How have your parents influenced the way you make decisions in your life? What have you learned from observing their decisions and the subsequent consequences? What decisions have you made in your life as a reaction against those of your parents? How have those turned out for you?

3. How often are you tempted to blame others for your problems or circumstances? When does this usually occur? What are the reasons you hold these other people responsible for what's going on in your own life?

4. How do you feel when you consider taking complete responsibility for the quality of your life? Angry at how unfair life can be? Fearful of having no one to blame but yourself? Annoyed by the question? Sad over the way you've blamed others in the past? Ashamed of your past mistakes? Other emotions?

5. If you were to take responsibility for your life, right now today, what's the first change you would make? If you were not afraid of the future or ashamed of your past, how would you like to change your life? What's kept you from making these changes so far? How have you handled these challenges?

"You"

Now that you have thought about the questions, honestly write out your answers below.

I tend to take too much responsibility for . . .

I do not take enough responsibility for . . .

_____

My attitude about responsibility has impacted my family members by . . .

_____

My attitude about responsibility has impacted others around me by . . .

_____

My parents influenced the way I make decisions in my life by . . .

_____

I learned from observing their decisions and the subsequent consequences that . . .

_____

Decisions I have made in my life as a reaction against those of my parents were . . .

_____

Those decision have turned out . . .

_____

I tend to blame others when . . .

_____

I hold these other people responsible for what's going on in my own life because . . .

_____

When I consider taking complete responsibility for the quality of my life, I feel . . .

_____

Were I to take responsibility for my life, right now, today, the first change I would make is . . .

_____

Were I not afraid of the future or ashamed of my past, I would change my life by . . .

_____

What's kept me from making these changes so far is . . .

_____

I have handled these challenges by . . .

_____

The blame game

Apply one word to each blank below. You may use each word only once.

Usually   Infrequently

Sometimes   Rarely

Occasionally   Almost never

I am _____ tempted to blame others for my problems or circumstances.

I am _____ angry at how unfair life can be.

I am _____ fearful of having no one to blame but myself.

I am _____ annoyed by the question that it might not be "their" fault.

I am _____ sad over the way I've blamed others in the past.

I am _____ ashamed of my past mistakes.

What do your responses say about your placement of blame on others? On yourself?

"Do"

The way to make any kind of change in your life is to begin with a vision. Considering how you want to feel and how you want your life to look is key to make lasting changes. Once you have a vision you can set out to make a plan.

Now that you've defined your values in Chapter One, the next step is to think about how you want to bring those values to life. You do that by having a vision for how you want to live, by taking responsibility for your life, right now, today.

From blame to aim—vision exercise

Consider the following question. If the world were perfect and you could do or be anything you wanted, what would your life look like? Begin fresh. You can return to the quiet place you found in Chapter One, or this might be a good time to sit with a cup of tea, light a candle, put on some smooth jazz or some other favorite music. Take a hot bubble bath or an extra-long shower. This is a chance to dream, let your imagination soar. Sit quietly and then write out whatever comes to you. Don't bring your old thoughts to the process. This is the new you making the list, the one who is not afraid of your future or ashamed of your past.

_____

_____

_____

_____

_____

_____

_____

_____

_____

_____

_____

_____

Consider what's kept *you* from making this vision a reality, so far, and write those factors down. Only write down "you" factors—not anything anyone else has contributed to stunting your vision.

_____

_____

_____

_____

_____

_____

_____

_____

_____

Now look at your list of hindrances. How many of them are real, such as "I have to take care of my elderly parents," versus how many are excuses—"My boss always keeps me late, and that's why I can't ever make it home for dinner with my wife and kids."

Now list things you can do to deal with these challenges when they come up in the future so that you can live more of the life you want. (For example, if the demands of your job keep you at the office late every night, but you value being an involved father and your vision is to be home for dinner before the kids go to bed, then perhaps you can arrange with your boss to leave in time for dinner and then do a few hours of work at home after the kids go to sleep.)

Consider the things you can do now to bring your vision to life. Think about some ways you can flip the script in your life and take more responsibility for getting what you need in your life.

My challenge   How I can flip the coin

_____   _____

_____   _____

_____   _____

_____   _____

_____   _____

Another great way to look at ways in your life where you have or haven't taken responsibility is to write your life history. Of course we aren't talking about a whole book here unless that is something you are really interested in doing. I am talking about going through your life decade by decade and noting some of the milestones or particularly difficult times.

This is a great time to pull out some old photo albums or letters and cards from friends, family, or old boyfriends or girlfriends. Read through them. What did you look like? Were you happy? Sad? Did you take a trip? Get married? Divorced? Doing this will spark memories you may have forgotten.

Write down happy times and sad times. Then, review each decade's entry and the memory of it and write down what you believe to be the reasons for what happened, good or bad.

Decade	Memory	Why it happened
1–10	_____	_____
11–20	_____	_____
21–30	_____	_____
31–40	_____	_____
41–50	_____	_____
51–60	_____	_____
61–70	_____	_____
71–80	_____	_____
81–90	_____	_____
91–100	_____	_____
100+	_____	_____

When you go over why it happened do you notice any patterns? If you have a lot of notations about so and so keeping you from . . . or so and so made you do *x*, or because of so and so you couldn't . . . you may not be taking enough responsibility in your life for what you do or don't do.

Parents are people, too—learn to stop blaming your parents

Parents in our society often get a bad rap. Whenever the kids get into trouble, the first people everyone blames are the parents. We often blame our parents much too much for failings that are our own individual responsibility.

There is no handbook for being a parent, no test you have to take, although sometimes it seems like there should be. Parents, like everyone, are, much as their children are, figuring out who they are as they go along. When we have the urge to blame our parents for everything that's wrong in our lives, it might be a better idea to stop and consider that they love us, want the best for us, and did the best they could.

How well do you really know your mother or father? If you are lucky enough to still have them with you on this earth consider a few ways that you might try to get to know them as people.

Invite your mom or dad to lunch or coffee—just the two of you. And rather than talk about what you are up to and your life, ask them questions about their life past and present. You'll be surprised at what you might learn. If you need some ideas, consider these questions:

- What did you like to study in school?
- Who were your friends?
- How did you meet Mom (or Dad)?
- What were your dreams as a child?
- What was your first job?
- What books did you read?

- How did you feel when I was born?
- What was your relationship with your parents?
- Did they encourage you to try new things?

These and other questions reveal much about our parents and who they were as people. Their answers will also reveal much about who they are now. If your father, for example, was forced to work in the family business when he really wanted to be a professional athlete, it could explain why he pushed you so much to play baseball when you'd have rather painted a picture. Understanding their past and the issues they had to deal with as people will go a long way to our having more compassion for the decisions they made with regard to us and some of the challenges they had to face while raising us. This way we'll be able to see them and the mistakes they made with us with a little more compassion. They are human beings just as we are and make mistakes just as we do. None of us is perfect.

If you have a tendency to blame your parents for what is wrong in your life, considering them in this light is the way to release yourself from a painful and disappointing past and allow space to focus on the future. When you focus less on blame and more on compassion, you can see the gift that exists in good and bad circumstances.

Look for the gift

Think of something you blame your parents for. For example, suppose your mother was fearful about being out late at night because she'd been mugged as a child on her way home from school. As a result she never let you go out to play with the other kids, and you spent a lot of time locked up in the house. What's the gift? Because you spent so much time alone, you became very independent and were able to entertain yourself without the help of others. Today, as a result of that independence and because you have little need to depend on the opinions of others, you have strong leadership and decision-making skills that have served you well in your professional career.

Are there some hidden gifts in circumstances for which you blamed your parents?

I blamed my parents for . . .   Now I see the hidden gift as . . .

_____   _____

_____   _____

_____   _____

_____   _____

_____   _____

Focusing only on what was wrong in your childhood will only leave you frustrated and stuck in the past. You often hear people say, "I don't want to be like my mother or my father." But then you see them doing exactly that! When you stay focused on the past, on blame, and on what was wrong, you continue to repeat many of the same mistakes.

Look forward in your life. Acknowledge what didn't work in the past that you'd like to do differently. Forgive your parents and know they did the best they knew how. Then look to your future with the understanding that you can accept all of who you are, good and bad, and move ahead.

Say "thank you"

Send you mom or dad a card or letter and thank them for all they've done for you. Acknowledge them for who they are as people and thank them for their influence in your becoming the person you are today. We aren't responsible for choosing our parents, but we are responsible for being the people we eventually become.

Change is hard. You can't expect to go from doing something one way for years—like blaming others—and then one day waking up and doing it differently.

You are going to have setbacks and challenges. Some days you are going to forget your new vow to take responsibility for your decisions and your life, and you are going to fall back into habitual, destructive patterns. Some days, you may even think that change is impossible. When you have a day like this, the key is for you to get back up, dust yourself off, and start again. Life is a marathon, not a sprint. Stay the course.

Every day, renew your enthusiasm to take responsibility for your life by sitting down and reviewing your list, praying, asking God to give you the strength to be the best person you can be, and asking for forgiveness on the days you slip back. Soon you will begin to see your life unfold in ways you never imagined.

three

Getting Rid of Emotional, Physical, and Spiritual Clutter

> *Before you begin this portion of the* Making Great Decisions Workbook, *read Chapter Three, "Before You Leave Junk in Your Trunk—Clean Up Emotionally"* (pages 47–62), *in* Making Great Decisions *(formerly titled* Before You Do*).*

Junk just accumulates as we live our lives until we realize that there's not enough room for the items we *do* wish to take with us. Often we drive nice cars, wear fashionable clothes, and live in stylish homes. However, the outside doesn't show you what is on the inside. It reminds me of what Jesus said about the Pharisees. He said that outside they were clean but inside they were full of dead men's bones (Matthew 23:27–29).

I know some *people* who look far better on the outside than on the inside. Alas, they have junk in the trunk, the kind that smells in a relationship and undermines what could have been, because they refuse to discard what used to be—they refuse to discard what was.

If you are going to make great decisions that leave you with no regrets, then you must clean out the junk in your trunk, let go of the past. Doing so will provide you the necessary space to see, breathe, and maneuver. You often won't know what you have; let alone what you need, in your life until you can clear the mental and emotional room to experience the here and now.

"Before" (Questions for Contemplation)

Follow the same process as in the previous chapters; reflect on all the questions before you write answers to any of them.

1. How much junk do you presently have in your trunk? Are you the kind of person who tends to dispose of items on a regular basis and prefers a neat and tidy environment? Or are you like my friend who couldn't fit my luggage into his car trunk because he carried around so many odds and ends?

2. How often do you hold grudges or hang on to past mistakes, even your own? When was the last time you felt like your mental and emotional "house" was clean and in order? What keeps you from "housecleaning" on a regular basis?

3. Who could you ask for help in identifying the junk in your life right now?

4. What's the greatest burden in your life right now? How can you remove it from your trunk? Sometimes we need help with the heavy lifting. Who could help you deal with the weight of this burden?

5. As you look forward to where you would like to go with your life, what will you need in order to get there? More education? Financial support for a new business? Encouragement from a mentor? Think through what you need to get rid of in your life so that you can make room for what you need to add in order to reach your destination.

"You"

Now that you have thought about the questions, honestly write out your answers below.

I define my "emotional junk" as _____ .

I presently have _____ in the hidden places of my life.

_____ can't fit in my life because I carry around so much junk.

The last time I felt like my mental and emotional house was clean and in order was _____ .

What keeps me from housecleaning on a regular basis is

_____ .

I could ask _____ for help in identifying the junk in my life right now.

The greatest burden in my life right now is _____ .

I could remove that burden by _____

_____ could help me deal with the weight of this burden.

To have the life I want, I will need _____ in order to get there.

To have the life I want, I will need to get rid of _____ in order to get there.

True junk dealers

Mark "True" or "False" for each sentence below:

_____ I am the kind of person who sees no reason to dispose of items on a regular basis.

_____ I am the kind of person who feels a neat and tidy environment is not lived in.

_____ I am the kind of person who holds grudges.

_____ I am the kind of person who hangs on to past mistakes others have made.

_____ I am the kind of person who hangs on to my own past mistakes.

If you marked "True" for any sentence, you need to check your trunk.

"Do"

Kinds of junk: physical and mental/emotional

There are two different kinds of junk—physical and mental/emotional—and both kinds of junk can weigh you down.

Physical junk is easy to get rid of

Physical junk is the kind we accumulate in the backs of closets, in those junk drawers where we can never quickly find a pen when we need to write a note or matches when the power goes out, or in our home office where we can never find the tax records or the immunization cards for the school trip, or the garage where we can never put our hands on the citronella candles to keep the mosquitoes at bay.

It is hard to function in an environment that isn't neat and organized. In fact, living with physical junk in your home is chaotic and spills out into other aspects of your life. Because you can't ever find the car keys in the morning you are always late to work, which could lead to your appearing unprofessional, or worse, could lead to losing your job.

Physical junk is not only annoying to step over and try to live around, but it takes away from the quality of your life and that of your family's. Give yourself twenty-five points for each activity below. Your goal is one hundred!

■ Purge and organize activity: If you have a family, make it like a game. Assign rooms or zones to family members and make them responsible for keeping their area neat. Give fun nonmonetary awards to the keeper of the neatest area.

■ Hire a company like 1–800-JUNK to literally come and take your junk away. Or schedule a pickup with organizations like The Salvation Army or Goodwill, or visit your local church or homeless shelter and donate clothing, shoes, books, and furniture. Not only are you getting rid of the physical junk from your space but you are also doing something good for someone else, giving what you don't need or use to someone who does.

■ Implement the one-in-one-out rule in your house. Any purchase you make to bring something into the house must be accompanied by giving or throwing something else away. This way clutter is less likely to accumulate.

■ Spend your free time volunteering to help people who have very little, rather than shopping for new things. Rebuilding houses on the Gulf Coast after Katrina, for example, is a surefire way to reassess what's important in life. So many people there lost all of their worldly possessions; what was important for them was that they survived.

■ Before you make any purchase ask yourself, "Do I really need this?" Walk away and wait twenty-four hours before you buy it. Most times you will find that it's a purchase that's unnecessary.

■ Figure out the hourly wage cost of an item that you wish to purchase. For example, say you see a beautiful pair of Jimmy Choo shoes that cost $500. Let's say you make $44,000 per year. Based on a forty-hour workweek at twenty days a month, you earn a little more than $18 an hour. That means you would have to work more than twenty-seven hours to earn the money for those Jimmy Choos. Perhaps a trip to Payless makes more sense?

■ Call a professional organizer, a feng shui specialist, or an honest, straightforward friend, and let them help you identify items that no longer serve you and help you let them go. Sometimes we've let things go on too long and the problem is just too big for us to handle on our own.

Any four of the above will give you a perfect score, and you'll be on your way to getting rid of the physical junk—a good start to working on the mental and emotional!

How to get rid of mental and emotional junk

Mental and emotional junk is made up of the regrets we have about past mistakes, the grudges we hold when we feel we've been done wrong, or the hurts we hide under clouds of anger, cynicism, and reclusiveness. Mental and emotional junk, while you can't literally see it, can weigh you down, as well. If you are the type to hold grudges or hang on to past mistakes, even your own, then you know the feeling of being weighed down by mental and emotional junk.

It is hard for a relationship to survive when either party hasn't processed their mental and emotional junk. Like blame, this junk keeps you stuck in the past. If an old beau has hurt you and you've never let that hurt go, each time your mate does something similar you will react, probably with unwarranted fervor, as if they were the original person who hurt you. The new mate is left feeling upset and confused at your over-the-top reaction to a small infraction that on its own was insignificant.

Make a junk list

Based on your thoughts and responses to the questions and exercises above, make a list of all the junk that's cluttering your trunk right now. Categorize your junk into the following kinds:

Junk from the Past, including events that you continue to replay, toxic relationships that you cling to, and emotions such as guilt, anger, and fear that need release.

_____   _____

_____   _____

_____   _____

_____   _____

_____   _____

Present Junk, which includes responsibilities you've taken on that are not essential or primary to your commitments, let alone your well-being.

_____   _____

_____   _____

_____   _____

_____   _____

_____   _____

Junk I'm Saving for the Future, which amounts to anxiety over change, dreams of life support, and worry about future outcomes over which you have no control.

_____   _____

_____   _____

_____   _____

_____   _____

_____   _____

Here are a few activities that might help you remain aware of your emotions and feelings and, rather than stuffing them inside, help you process issues as they arise.

Tell a friend

There is no substitute for open and honest communication. When issues do come up, it's best to talk to those you are in a relationship with in kindness, truth, and honesty. That old adage "Love means never going to bed angry" is a good motto for keeping mental and emotional junk where it belongs—out of your trunk and in the trash.

Review your list above and identify a friend who might be a good confidant to help you unburden. Not every friend will understand every issue. Note below which friend can help with which issue.

Issue   Friend

_____   _____

_____   _____

_____   _____

_____   _____

_____   _____

Pray

If you have something you regret, something that you have been wrestling with, or something that you believe is keeping you stuck, turn to the Lord and pray. Make your prayer list using the emotional junk items from your You list above.

_____   _____

_____   _____

_____   _____

_____   _____

Word your prayers specifically for what you need to see, learn, etc. Remember, prayer is not just asking God, but making commitments to God; apologizing, if need be; asking for forgiveness; and asking to be set free. Write your prayer here.

_____   _____

_____   _____

_____   _____

_____   _____

_____   _____

Set a time to pray this prayer regularly during the next thirty days and record what you experience from your prayers.

Sun	Mon	Tues	Wed	Thu	Fri	Sat
1	2	3	4	5	6	7
8	9	10	11	12	13	14
15	16	17	18	19	20	21
22	23	24	25	26	27	28
29	30					

Prayer session

Prayer experience

_____

_____

_____

_____

_____

_____

_____

_____

_____

_____

_____

_____

_____

_____   _____

_____   _____

_____   _____

_____   _____

_____   _____

_____   _____

_____   _____

_____   _____

_____   _____

_____   _____

_____   _____

_____   _____

Spend some time in prayer over each of the three kinds of junk and release them to the God who can restore order to even the messiest of houses. Allow the Spirit to cleanse you from the inside out. Ask the Almighty for wisdom about how to move forward in your life. Be willing to act on what you discern in your prayers. Now let go of that junk in your trunk and travel lighter than you have in years! You will feel the mental clutter fade away and peace begin to wash over you.

Journal

I've asked you to note your thoughts and feelings throughout the Questions for Contemplation section of this book. You've probably noticed how patterns have emerged in terms of your thoughts, feelings, and actions. Journaling can be a very cathartic activity and very effective at getting clearer about feelings and issues. Choose a nice book, but nothing so nice that you are afraid to write in it! Then set aside time, as little as five minutes on a regular basis, and write and write and write some more. Keep it in a safe place so you feel free to really express yourself for no one but you. And don't censor yourself. This is your chance to express how you really, truly feel without prettying it up. Let loose. You'll begin to feel lighter and freer instantly.

Meditate

"Be still and know that I am God" (Psalm 46:10). Like prayer, meditation is a powerful tool for releasing us from our emotional clutter. It forces you to sit in quiet and silence your thoughts.

Using your same emotional junk list from the You exercise in this chapter *or* your prayer list above, pick a Scripture that corresponds to each junky item. Choose a verse or verses that promise victory and encourage you.

Mental/Emotional junk   Scripture

_____   _____

_____   _____

_____   _____

_____   _____

_____   _____

_____   _____

_____   _____

Memorize and meditate on each passage of Scripture.

Exercise

Some have called exercise "sweating prayers." Exercise releases toxins and stress and improves your mood almost immediately. It can also be a great time to concentrate on God and Scripture. Just walking as little as thirty minutes a day can go a long way to releasing emotional tension and allow you to have calmer, more focused discussions.

Use your junk list from the prayer or meditation activities above to create an exercise regimen where you work on releasing your emotional and mental junk. For example, if you take a dance class every Thursday evening, commit yourself to focusing on a particular element of your mental and emotional junk—say, releasing a grudge against an old boyfriend—with every kick or jump. The same applies to your time on the treadmill, stationary bike, or life cycle. Your moves can be powerful emotional releases.

Exercise   Mental/Emotional junk to release

_____   _____

_____   _____

_____   _____

_____   _____

_____   _____

_____

Visit a clergy member or consider therapy

If there are issues you feel are affecting your daily life and your relationships and that remain after a season of concentrated prayer, meditation, and balanced exercise, or if your emotional issues are forcing you to be reclusive or perpetually angry, or if you feel you might be depressed or have other emotional issues, talk with a member of your clergy or a mental health professional such as a therapist or counselor, or join a support group. There is no shame in seeking mental health support, and results can be transformative. To have an unbiased, supportive ear to which we can bare our innermost feelings is often the first step toward healing emotional issues.

Mental/Emotional junk unreleased

_____

_____

_____

Talking is often the best way to purge painful mental and emotional junk. Knowing that there are others who understand your feelings and support you unconditionally can be very cathartic and lighten the burden of carrying all that junk!

four
Take the Lead
Determining Your Leadership Style

Before you begin this portion of the Making Great Decisions Workbook, *read Chapter Four, "Before You Lead— Decide on Your Team" (pages 63–81), in* Making Great Decisions *(formerly titled* Before You Do*).*

Begin to think of yourself as a CEO, as a leader, the one who makes decisions about your life. Your team members are those whose contributions affect the quality of your life. Consider this understanding of ownership and stewardship: God is your owner, and you have dominion; the earth is the Lord's, but God hands us humans the task of running it. God owns your life, but you care for it. This gives you the power to make the necessary decisions in your life.

"Before" (Questions for Contemplation)

Follow the same process as in the previous chapters. And be sure to keep your pen nearby.

1. Do you tend to think of yourself as a leader? Why or why not? Do you lead more at work or at home?

2. How would you describe your natural leadership style? How involved or immersed in the details of a project do you like to be? Are you more of a big-picture visionary leader or someone who gets hands-on and works from the ground up?

3. How well have you handled conflicts and controversy in your past leadership roles? What have you learned from these experiences?

4. What's your greatest strength or asset as a leader? Your greatest weakness? Have you surrounded yourself with others who complement your strengths and weaknesses? In what areas do you need more support—administration, delegation, execution, evaluation, etc.?

5. Do you have more confidants, constituents, or comrades in your life at present? Be as specific as possible identifying in which categories those around you best fit. Which area needs to have more members?

"You"

Everyone leads in some way, to some extent. On the chart below evaluate your leadership, using numbers ranging from 1 to 5, with 1 meaning the statement is extremely true of you and 5 being least true of you.

	1	2	3	4	5
I tend to think of myself as a leader.					
I lead more at work.					
I lead more at home.					
I am a natural leader.					

	1	2	3	4	5
I have had to develop my leadership style.					
I like to know but not be involved in the details of a project.					
I dislike being immersed in the fine details of a project.					
I am more of a big-picture visionary leader.					
I am someone who lets others get hands-on and work from the ground up.					
I handle conflicts well in my leadership roles.					
I handle controversy well in my leadership roles.					
I have learned a lot about leadership from my experiences.					
I have surrounded myself with others who complement me as a leader.					
My score: _____					

The lower your score, the more developed you currently are as a CEO-leader of your life, one who makes decisions about your life.

Styles of leadership vary as much as types of leaders. Some leaders are detail oriented; they are hands-on, and they like to work from the ground up and be immersed in and informed of every aspect of a project or activity. Others are more big picture and visionary; they leave the details to those who report to them, relying on the expertise of others to help them toward their goals. Home in on your specific leadership gifts and areas that need development by filling in these statements, based on your Before reflections above.

My greatest strength as a leader is _____ .

My greatest asset as a leader is _____ .

My greatest weakness as a leader is _____ .

If you are staring blankly at these lines, use the prompts below to help you.

My greatest strength as a leader is:

     Administration

     Delegation

     Execution

     Evaluation

     Other _____

I need more support as a leader in:

     Administration

     Delegation

     Execution

     Evaluation

     Other _____

My leadership team

List the team in your life at present under the following three categories. Be as specific as possible in identifying the categories in which those around you best fit.

Confidants

_____

_____

_____

Constituents

_____

_____

_____

Comrades

_____

_____

_____

Which area needs to have more members?

_____

It is often a hard lesson to learn and often painful to accept, but no matter how good a person you are, not everyone in the world has you or your best interests at heart. Different types of people require different types of relationships. Work to determine to what level you should interact with people. Only certain people, and typically only a few, belong in your inner circle of confidants. If you're willing to be ruthlessly honest with yourself about the relationships in your life, then you will be poised to make the very best decisions. However, you must know who you're dealing with before you do. Carefully consider the relationships in your life. Now choose five to ten people who you consider on your leader ship team.

My leadership team

1. _____ _____

2. _____ _____

3. _____ _____

4. _____ _____

5. _____ _____

6. _____ _____

7. _____ _____

8. _____ _____

9. _____   _____

10. _____   _____

Consider your team members and their strengths. Thinking about this carefully will help you know who you can call on for help either now or in the future.

My leadership team   What they are good at
                                  (their strengths)

1. _____   _____

2. _____   _____

3. _____   _____

4. _____   _____

5. _____   _____

6. _____   _____

7. _____   _____

8. _____   _____

9. _____   _____

10. _____   _____

My leadership characteristics

All leaders have four basic characteristics. Score yourself using the following chart.

	Always 1	Usually 2	Sometimes 3	Never 4
A willingness to be controversial				
A belief that decisions create conflict				
A sense of commitment				
An assurance of being guided by one's character				

Scoring:

4–6 = Congratulations—you are the CEO-leader of your life.

7–8 = You are on your way to becoming the CEO-leader of your life.

9–11 = You are becoming aware of the need to be the CEO-leader of your life.

12–16 = Becoming the CEO-leader of your life needs to be a high priority
        for you.

If you scored 12 or higher, you must understand that you are the leader of your life and move away from being a peacemaker to being a policy maker. Your goal is not to keep peace but to develop policies. It is rarely an easy job or one that necessarily makes you very popular. If you don't consider yourself a leader, perhaps you are not taking responsibility for the decisions you make in your life and are relying too much on others to lead the way.

Conduct your own 360

This week, ask people around you to give you specific feedback about how they view your leadership style. Choose individuals who know you in different roles—work, home, church, school, the gym, etc.

Feedback giver #1 _____

On the chart below evaluate my leadership, using numbers ranging from 1 to 5, with 1 meaning the statement is extremely true of me and 5 being least true of me. Be completely honest. Do not be afraid to hurt my feeling. Proverbs 27:6 says, "Wounds from a friend can be trusted . . ." Your honest feedback, even if it hurts, will help me grow.

	1	2	3	4	5
You think of me as a leader.					
I lead in the situations in which you see me.					
You see me as a natural leader.					
You have seen me develop my leadership style.					
You see me as needing to know but not involved in the details of a project.					
You see me being immersed in the fine details of a project.					
You see me as a big-picture visionary leader.					
You see me as someone who lets others get hands-on and work from the ground up.					
You see me handle conflicts well in my leadership roles.					
You see me handle controversy well in my leadership roles.					
You see that I have learned a lot about leadership from my experiences.					
You see that I have surrounded myself with others who complement me as a leader.					

My score: _____

Feedback giver #2 _____

On the chart below evaluate my leadership, using numbers ranging from 1 to 5, with 1 meaning the statement is extremely true of me and 5 being least true of me. Be completely honest. Do not be afraid to hurt my feeling. Proverbs 27:6 says, "Wounds from a friend can be trusted . . ." Your honest feedback, even if it hurts, will help me grow.

	1	2	3	4	5
You think of me as a leader.					
I lead in the situations in which you see me.					
You see me as a natural leader.					
You have seen me develop my leadership style.					
You see me as needing to know but not involved in the details of a project.					
You see me being immersed in the fine details of a project.					
You see me as a big-picture visionary leader.					
You see me as someone who lets others get hands-on and work from the ground up.					
You see me handle conflicts well in my leadership roles.					
You see me handle controversy well in my leadership roles.					
You see that I have learned a lot about leadership from my experiences.					
You see that I have surrounded myself with others who complement me as a leader.					
My score: _____					

Feedback giver #3 _____

On the chart below evaluate my leadership, using numbers ranging from 1 to 5, with 1 meaning the statement is extremely true of me and 5 being least true of me. Be completely honest. Do not be afraid to hurt my feeling. Proverbs 27:6 says, "Wounds from a friend can be trusted . . ." Your honest feedback, even if it hurts, will help me grow.

	1	2	3	4	5
You think of me as a leader.					
I lead in the situations in which you see me.					
You see me as a natural leader.					
You have seen me develop my leadership style.					
You see me as needing to know but not involved in the details of a project.					
You see me being immersed in the fine details of a project.					
You see me as a big-picture visionary leader.					
You see me as someone who lets others get hands-on and work from the ground up.					
You see me handle conflicts well in my leadership roles.					
You see me handle controversy well in my leadership roles.					
You see that I have learned a lot about leadership from my experiences.					
You see that I have surrounded myself with others who complement me as a leader.					
My score: _____					

Feedback giver #4 _____

On the chart below evaluate my leadership, using numbers ranging from 1 to 5, with 1 meaning the statement is extremely true of me and 5 being least true of me. Be completely honest. Do not be afraid to hurt my feeling. Proverbs 27:6 says, "Wounds from a friend can be trusted . . ." Your honest feedback, even if it hurts, will help me grow.

	1	2	3	4	5
You think of me as a leader.					
I lead in the situations in which you see me.					
You see me as a natural leader.					
You have seen me develop my leadership style.					
You see me as needing to know but not involved in the details of a project.					
You see me being immersed in the fine details of a project.					
You see me as a big-picture visionary leader.					
You see me as someone who lets others get hands-on and work from the ground up.					
You see me handle conflicts well in my leadership roles.					
You see me handle controversy well in my leadership roles.					
You see that I have learned a lot about leadership from my experiences.					
You see that I have surrounded myself with others who complement me as a leader.					

My score: _____

Feedback giver #5 _____

On the chart below evaluate my leadership, using numbers ranging from 1 to 5, with 1 meaning the statement is extremely true of me and 5 being least true of me. Be completely honest. Do not be afraid to hurt my feeling. Proverbs 27:6 says, "Wounds from a friend can be trusted . . ." Your honest feedback, even if it hurts, will help me grow.

	1	2	3	4	5
You think of me as a leader.					
I lead in the situations in which you see me.					
You see me as a natural leader.					
You have seen me develop my leadership style.					
You see me as needing to know but not involved in the details of a project.					
You see me being immersed in the fine details of a project.					
You see me as a big-picture visionary leader.					
You see me as someone who lets others get hands-on and work from the ground up.					
You see me handle conflicts well in my leadership roles.					
You see me handle controversy well in my leadership roles.					
You see that I have learned a lot about leadership from my experiences.					
You see that I have surrounded myself with others who complement me as a leader.					
My score: _____					

Overall 360 Feedback score:

Feedback giver #1 score: _____

Feedback giver #2 score: _____

Feedback giver #3 score: _____

Feedback giver #4 score: _____

Feedback giver #5 score: _____

TOTAL score: _____

The lower your score, the more developed you are currently viewed by others as a leader and a CEO-leader of your life, one who makes decisions about your life. Consider how you can recalibrate your leadership style based on the responses from those who know you best.

What common themes emerge from the various individuals?

_____

_____

What surprised you the most about their feedback?

_____

_____

What hurt the most?

_____

_____

What encouraged or helped you the most?

_____

_____

"Do" _____

My leadership style

You can be a leader at home and/or at work. Leadership does not only apply to people in positions of power such as presidents or corporate CEOs. You show leadership in the way you choose to live your life, the way you interact with others no matter what their social status, and the example you set for your family, friends, and others you come into contact with. Consider taking a small step each day this week to show leadership at home or at work.

The top five policies in my home are . . .

_____

_____

_____

_____

_____

The policies that are not being practiced at home in the way I prefer are . . .

_____

_____

_____

_____

_____

A new policy I wish to implement in my home is . . .

_____

The top five policies in my workplace are . . .

_____

_____

_____

_____

_____

The policies that are not being practiced at work in the way I prefer are . . .

_____

_____

_____

_____

_____

A new policy I wish to implement at work is . . .

_____

I can show leadership to my significant other by . . .

_____

I can show leadership to my kids by . . .

_____

I can show leadership to my coworkers by . . .

_____

I can show leadership to my community by . . .

_____

five

Join Right

Associating Wisely

> *Before you begin this portion of the* Making Great Decisions Workbook, *read Chapter Five, "Before You Join" (pages 83–94), in* Making Great Decisions *(formerly titled* Before You Do*).*

Making the decision to commit ourselves to affiliate with a group, institution, program, club, or any group of individuals, whether it's a church in our community, a professional organization of our peers, a country club for those who have arrived, or a group devoted to a shared hobby or passion, requires due diligence similar to any other major decision.

"Before" (Questions for Contemplation)

Follow the same reflection process as in the previous chapters, keeping your pen handy.

1. What are the organizations to which you currently belong? How long have you been involved with each of them? How did you first join each of them? How many of them are exclusive, with specific criteria for membership? How many can anyone join? Which type do you tend toward in your life?

2. How have you benefited from the various affiliations you have? What has been the cost of each, in dollars as well as time and energy? Which ones no longer serve your present needs or season of life?

3. How have you usually approached the decision about church involvement or membership? How well does your present place of worship serve the needs of you and your family? Is it time to consider a different kind of church community?

4. What's the most exclusive group of which you are a member? How did you attain membership? How did you view this group prior to becoming a member? After being a member? Would you join it again or advise others to join?

5. What's the group, organization, or institution to which you wish you presently belonged? What has kept you from joining? What other commitments would you need to give up in order to join this new affiliation?

"You"—Why Join?

You must be careful not to expect too much from your affiliation with the group, but you must also have solid expectations about what it will deliver. As selfish as this may sound, the most important question you can ask before you join any group is "How will this feed me?"

Write your answer here:

_____

_____

_____

Reasons to join must include a tangible benefit, an intangible satisfaction, or a future return. Place a check next to the statements that apply to you.

_____ To help my career

_____ To meet certain people

_____ To get certain perks

_____ To feed me spiritually

_____ For enjoyment

_____ Other gain _____

Assess the level of your involvement in each group you already belong to, and next to each one write how you feel about belonging to it at this time in your life: great, OK, pressured, frustrated, bad, etc. Identify the associations that can be severed and take immediate steps to terminate your membership and responsibilities. You will feel lighter and less encumbered and in turn able to turn your attention to other affiliations that will feed your present needs more effectively.

Affiliations with clubs, organizations, committees	Level of commitment (high, moderate, low, none)	Feelings about membership (great, OK, necessary, frustrated, bad, etc.)

Why did you join? Why do you stay?

As social beings we like to belong; it's human nature. But often belonging becomes more about social status than giving back, helping, or whatever your original altruistic intent was. Consider the organizations you currently belong to and make a list. How long you've been involved with each of them. Why you joined in the first place. Now on a scale from 1 to 10, rate how close your reasons for joining are to the reasons you now stay, with 10 being the same and 1 being not the same at all.

Organization	Why I joined	Rating
1. _____	_____	_____
2. _____	_____	_____
3. _____	_____	_____
4. _____	_____	_____
5. _____	_____	_____
6. _____	_____	_____
7. _____	_____	_____
8. _____	_____	_____

The types of organizations you tend to join can reveal a lot about what is important to you. If the reasons you joined in the first place still hold true, then you should probably remain a member and keep doing what you're doing. But if you find you rate many of the organizations on your list as 3, 2, or 1, they may no longer serve your present needs or season of life, and could be costing you a great deal in financial commitments and time and energy. It may be time to reassess your affiliations.

What you can uniquely contribute

The other questions you must ask yourself before you join are:

What can I uniquely contribute?

_____

What do I have to offer that no one else can contribute, that makes me irreplaceable to the group?

_____

If you're staring blankly at the fill-in lines, use this list to get your juices flowing:

Dollars/Money	Passion for the cause
Time	Ability to enable
Talents for the topic	

"Do"—Learn from Past Joining Mistakes

Make a list of all your affiliations: the clubs, organizations, and committees to which you belong. Be as comprehensive as possible in making your list—include everything from professional organizations to sororities and fraternities, committees at church or school, the choir or deacon board, the local homeowners' board in your neighborhood, the aerobics squad at the gym, or the election committee for your county representative. Next to each write out your level of commitment to that group—high, moderate, low, none.

Other groups in which I am a nominal member:

_____

_____

_____

Other groups that I feel are yet another obligation:

_____

_____

_____

Other groups that I feel are commitments that are weights around my neck:

_____

_____

_____

Look back to your list of values in Chapter One (page 6). Now think about the group or organization you wish to join. This is an excellent way to test whether your desired group is really something you want to be a part of. Use the chart below to note whether its values are compatible with yours. You won't be happy over the long term if you are part of an organization that conflicts with who you truly are as a person.

Your list of values (from Chapter One)	Organization you desire to join	What organization stands for	Similarities with organizations you already belong to	Conflicts with organizations you already belong to

As your needs change, don't be afraid to cut ties to former organizations that may have served you well in the past but that no longer meet your current needs.

six

Create Your Support Team
Success Is a Team Sport

Before you begin this portion of the Making Great Decisions Workbook, *read Chapter Six, "Before You Decide
to Love" (pages 95–107), in* Making Great Decisions
(formerly titled Before You Do*).*

The decision to love is the hardest and easiest decision you'll ever make.
It's easy because when you love someone, the joy you experience in being
around that person is effortless. Yet there is always a cost of loving someone.
Let's count the cost in this workbook chapter.

"Before" (Questions for Contemplation)

Follow the same reflection process as in the previous chapters. Keep your pen
handy.

1. How often do you order merchandise online or from catalogs? Generally, how well
have your expectations been met regarding what you thought you ordered versus what
actually arrived? Does this analogy hold up with how you currently view romantic relationships? Why or why not?

2. How would you describe your current season of relational involvement? If you're married or in a committed relationship, how satisfied are you currently with the quality of this union? What do you enjoy most about this person? What's your greatest challenge to growing closer?

3. If you're in the dating game, how do you presently discern with whom you will go out? How often is this decision based on the other person's appearance and attractiveness? How often is it based on how this person makes you feel? What criteria are you presently neglecting that should be included in your selection process?

4. What's been your greatest relational disappointment so far in life? What did you learn from this experience? How has it prevented you from being vulnerable in your present relationships? What would it mean for you to risk loving someone again?

5. Knowing that we're all flawed human beings dependent on God's grace, what's your idea of the perfect partner? What would your ideal relationship look like? How far are you from where you want to be in such a relationship? What needs to happen for your ideal to become reality?

"You"—Admit You Want a Relationship

Go back to the questions above and free-associate your answers by writing down any words that come to your mind as you contemplate the questions. Your list might look like this:

content . . . courage . . . disappointed . . . dry . . . exceeded . . . excited . . . full . . . hunches . . . intimacy . . . loving . . . personality . . . physical . . . physical attraction . . . pleasantly surprised . . . resilience . . . romantic . . . sparse . . . wowed!

Now, look at your free-associative words and circle the *two* words that most express your hopes for a relationship.

Next, be honest with yourself about wanting a relationship. Mark the following statements "True" or "False," based on how you honestly feel.

_____ No matter how successful I am, it matters who I come home to.

_____ I wonder about companionship when I retire.

_____ I want someone to travel with.

_____ When I see those older couples holding hands, I feel envious.

_____ I wonder who will walk beside me when my hair is silver and my gait is slower.

Put a check next to the statements that apply to you.

When someone first meets me, what they likely notice first is my . . .

___ body thickness   ___ height

___ body thinness   ___ shape/size of legs

___ breast/chest size   ___ skin color

___ buttocks shape/size   ___ weight

___ hair texture or color

Changes I need to make in my physical appearance (write your response below):

_____

_____

_____

_____

You are what you attract

In Question 5 above I asked you to think about your idea of the perfect partner and what your ideal relationship would look like. Now consider who you are, and whether you are the kind of person who would attract such a partner, and make a list of qualities . . .

I seek in a partner	I possess fully	I possess in part	I do not possess

Over the next week, call five friends whom you trust to be honest with you and ask them to list three great things about you. Easy. And then, do something a little harder. Ask them three things you could work on.

Friend #1
Three great things about me

_____

_____

_____

Three things I could work on

_____

_____

_____

Friend #2
Three great things about me

_____

_____

_____

Three things I could work on

_____

_____

_____

Friend #3
Three great things about me

_____

_____

_____

Three things I could work on

_____

_____

_____

Friend #4
Three great things about me

_____

_____

_____

Three things I could work on

_____

_____

_____

Friend #5
Three great things about me

_____

_____

_____

Three things I could work on

_____

_____

_____

When they tell you the three things you could work on, be quiet. The object of this exercise is to take in information, to listen. This is not a chance for you to justify anything, prove anything, or state your case. Take in the information they give, write it down, and say nothing in response except to thank them for their feedback. Use the chart below to summarize what your friends say.

Likable things about me	Things I must work on	Things I need to clarify

Their answers will give you clues about how people see you, good and bad. If your friends see them, so will your potential significant other.

Vow to consider the bad things, and think about what you might do to work on adjusting the negative part of your image.

Things I must work on	One way I will work in this	A second way I will work on this

"Do"

We've all had relationships that didn't work out for one reason or another. Perhaps we made mistakes that drove our partner away, or maybe our significant other treated us wrongly. The loss of a relationship can be a traumatic experience and can affect us in our lives for weeks, months, and sometimes years. The key to moving on from the end of a relationship is not to focus on what went wrong or to blame our partner for what we perceive to be their mistakes or shortcomings. Rather, when a relationship ends, our task is to determine what lessons we can learn from the experience so as not to repeat it the next time around.

In a recent interview on the Sundance Channel program *Iconoclasts,* Dr. Maya Angelou said it best: "It takes courage to love somebody; you have to risk everything." No matter what has happened to you, the only hope of a healthy future relationship is to let go of the past.

Write a letter

Make a list of all the people you have had relationships with that ended prematurely. It could be a friend, a lover, a spouse, a relative, or a coworker, or even someone who perhaps died with unfinished business between you. Then consider writing a letter to the person or persons and include the following:

1. Mention things that you liked or admired about them that initially drew you into the relationship.

2. Apologize for anything you might have done to hurt them and ask for forgiveness for yourself. You need to understand what role you played in the relationship's demise, and work to come to peace with your partner's behavior as well as your own.

3. Let them know that you forgive them for things they may have done to you. And express understanding for choices they may have made or actions they took.

4. Tell them one thing that you always meant to tell them but never got the chance.

5. Wish them the best with where they are with their lives and thank them for teaching you whatever lesson you learned from them.

Dear _____ ,

Yours truly,

_____ *(Fill in your name)*

If perhaps you wish to reconnect with a person, then you might want to mail the letter. But it isn't necessary to do so; that is not necessarily the point of this exercise. The idea is for you to release your feelings of hurt or resentment. This is the only way to truly move forward. Carrying around old hurts and leftover resentments keeps you from being open to prospective interactions and prevents you from being fully vulnerable so that you can step into your next relationship free of ties to your past.

Write an ad for your ideal relationship

Imagine that you are writing a personals ad for an ideal relationship with Mr. or Miss Right. Write as much as possible to describe the kind of relationship you would like to enjoy. What would it look like on a daily basis? How would you handle conflict? What kinds of activities would you do together? Be as specific as possible. Now, based on your description, write your ad and limit yourself to one hundred words. This will help you focus and prioritize what you really desire in a long-term committed relationship.

Ad headline: _____

One-hundred-word ad copy:

_____

_____

_____

_____

_____

_____

_____

_____

_____

_____

_____

_____

_____

_____

_____

_____

_____

_____

_____

Do ask . . .

The steps you have taken so far in this book will contribute to healthier partnerships in the future. Once you decide you are really ready for a relationship you must go about finding that special someone. Here are a few things to try that might help you connect with Mr. or Miss Right.

1. Friends and Family. The people who know you best are often a great source to help you find a potential mate.

Friends
Three friends I can ask to introduce me to new people

_____

_____

_____

Family
Three family members I can ask to introduce me to new people

_____

_____

_____

2. Work. Work can be a place to meet people. Tread carefully, however. You don't want to rush into a relationship with a coworker and then have it end badly. Think of work situations where you can meet new people, not those you work with. Conferences, off-site meetings, and special projects are all great meeting opportunities.

Three work-related settings where I might meet new people

_____

_____

_____

3. Hobbies and interests. Pursue the things you love and love will find you. If you are a singer, join a choir, attend concerts, or take a music appreciation class. If you are a runner, join a running club, enter a race, or attend a lecture on healthy eating for runners. You are sure to enjoy yourself at events related to things you are already interested in, and there will be others in attendance with whom you already have something in common. See someone you think is attractive, go over and introduce yourself to them, strike up a conversation. Even if you don't make a love connection, you may find yourself a new friend with similar interests.

Three fun-related settings where I might meet new people

_____

_____

_____

4. Be alone. Eat, walk, shop by yourself. If you want a relationship you can't travel in packs. Women in particular do this. Friends are great; they are vital to a happy life, but most men would rather have a root canal than approach a group of women. Take a chance and be alone. And if your goal is to meet someone, leave the book or newspaper at home. No one can strike up a conversation with you if your eyes are locked on

the text. Look around, notice who comes in, practice smiling and making eye contact with people.

Three settings where I can be comfortably alone and might meet new people

_____

_____

_____

seven

Choose and Be Chosen
Be the Partner You Hope to Find

> *Before you begin this portion of the* Making Great Decisions Workbook, *read Chapter Seven, "Before You Place Your Love Order" (pages 109–120), in* Making Great Decisions *(formerly titled* Before You Do*).*

He may look perfect from his profile online. She might seem like your soul mate because of the incredible compatibility determined by your twenty-nine personality trait tests. Online dating sites and community chat rooms have given a whole new dimension to male order! However, there is no substitute for the real thing. In fact, I have found that many people are excellent daters. They are so extremely proficient at dating that they are almost professionals. They know how to impress you really well for a night, a concert, or a weekend trip. But that doesn't mean that what you saw in the catalog is what you'll get in the male!

"Before" (Questions for Contemplation)

Follow the same process as in the previous chapters. And be sure and keep your pen and paper nearby.

1. How long have you known the person with whom you are presently in a relationship? How well do you think you know this person? What's the basis for your knowledge?

2. When was the last time you discussed your relational expectations with your date or spouse? What are you expecting from this person today? This week? This year? What prevents you from being more direct in sharing your expectations?

3. What's been the most surprising observation you've made about your present date or spouse? How has this person changed since you've met him or her?

4. How does your partner respond when you ask questions about him? How often does she ask you questions about yourself? On a scale of 1 to 10, how would you score the level of transparency you have with your partner, with 10 being totally open and honest?

5. How did you discover what you know about them? From what sources? How much effort have you spent verifying this person's character?

"You"

Go back to your list of values and what's important to you from Chapter One (page 6). Now consider the person you are thinking of dating and what they seem to value. Write it out below.

Value	How he or she practices/exhibits this value

_____   _____

_____   _____

"Do"—Choosing Someone to Date

If you are currently dating, discerning with whom you'd like to go out should be an active choice. While physical attraction and appearance are likely to be the first things we notice, looks soon fade. Focus on what you _really_ want in a partner.

Think honestly about their looks and write your thoughts down.

I like everything about how this person looks except

_____

The one thing I most like about the way this person looks is

_____

I like the way this person looks, but my friends will say

_____

I like the way this person looks now, but

_____

Evaluate your honest responses. Are there things that the person could already be working on correcting _or_ attitude changes _you_ need to make? Write your response below.

_____

This person's looks appeal most to my (circle one):

_____

Hormones   Eyes

Thinking about who is right for me   Status consciousness

Are there attitude changes *you* need to make? Write your response below.

_____

When I first meet someone, I consider their . . .

___ manners.

___ treatment of others, e.g., the restaurant waitstaff.

___ types of interests.

___ spiritual beliefs and if they share mine.

___ interest in what I have to say.

Are there attitude changes *you* need to make? Write your response below.

_____

When I first meet someone, I consider their . . .

___ height.

___ weight.

___ hair texture or color.

___ skin color.

___ body thinness.

___ body thickness.

___ breast/chest size.

___ buttocks shape/size.

___ legs shape/size.

Are there attitude changes *you* need to make? Write your response below.

_____

When I first meet someone, I consider their . . .

___ readiness to smile.

___ direct, open eye contact.

___ firm handshake.

___ presence.

___ willingness to flirt.

___ obvious availability.

Are there attitude changes *you* need to make? Write your response below.

_____

"Do" _____

Choose—don't just be chosen

Make sure you are the chooser and not the chosen, but recognize how you choose. Cross out all the ways of choosing on the list below that you feel are inappropriate. Circle all that remain, the ones that you use.

I show I want to meet a person by:

Asking a mutual acquaintance to introduce us.

Asking the person about something they've said, done, or are wearing.

Asking the person to get me a drink or do a similar social favor.

Asking the person to light a cigarette for me.

Complimenting the person on something I genuinely admire or like about them.

Displaying minor helplessness, distress, or need for assistance.

Easing into that person's space, hoping to get the person's attention.

Flashing my ability to spend big or showing opulence.

Flirting.

Getting in the person's face and making my interest known directly.

Giving them a firm handshake when I greet them.

Introducing myself at an opportune moment.

Making a scene, so the person has to notice me.

Making direct, open eye contact.

Making my presence known by walking or talking seductively.

Showing I am obviously available through sexual innuendo.

Smiling at them openly.

Staring at the person with attitude.

Striking up a conversation I know will interest the person.

Talking about myself, my accomplishments, my importance.

Touching the person seductively.

Improve your listening skills

Somewhere in the fine print of meeting, dating, and interacting with some- one, that person warns us ever so slightly that they are going to be a certain way. The red flags are always there. Learn to listen to the voice inside. As Maya Angelou says, "If someone tells you who they are, believe them."

Good and careful listening requires an active effort. Put other thoughts and concerns aside and focus on your partner. Take note of the words they say, the verbal cues as well as the nonverbal cues such as body language, eye contact, seeming nervous, etc. Don't try to think of answers to what your loved one is saying; simply focus on listening. Do more listening than talking. And while they are talking, consider these hints to get more out of the conversation:

- Put yourself in your partner's place as you listen.
- Don't interrupt.
- Write things down when they are talking to be sure you remember the important points.
- Look at your partner; face them when they are talking; make eye contact to show interest.
- Practice saying, "What I heard you say is . . ."

Rate yourself using this worksheet in your next few conversations. (It's especially easy to use in phone conversations!) Mark how you did with each item on the list.

Almost always   Occasionally/Infrequently

Usually/Frequently   Rarely/Almost never

_____ Put myself in my partner's place as I listened.

_____ Didn't interrupt.

_____ Wrote things down when they were talking to be sure I remembered the important points of what they said.

_____ Looked at my partner; faced them when they were talking; made eye contact to show interest.

_____ Practiced saying, "What I heard you say is . . ."

eight

Making Sure What Appears Is What Is

> *Before you begin this portion of the* Making Great Decisions Workbook, *read Chapter Eight, "Before You Commit—Research" (pages 121–134), in* Making Great Decisions *(formerly titled* Before You Do*).*

Before you can begin to scrutinize the other person, you must recognize your own limitations and your motivations for the relationship. Jesus asks us, "Why do you look at the speck of sawdust in your brother's eye and pay no attention to the plank in your own eye?" (Matthew 7:3). In other words, we must consider how we see ourselves before we can look closely at the other person in our life.

Self-image has so much to do with effective communication. When you see yourself as valuable enough to deserve love and attention from another person, then you form a boundary that you will not compromise. If this foundation of self-worth is not in place, then you become so grateful for any kind of love that you ignore the price. When this occurs, it's easy to make yourself a victim because you ignore warnings, overlook concerns, and deny reality. In many ways we end up getting what we deserve in relationships to which we have not applied the old adage, Caveat emptor—"Buyer beware."

"Before" (Questions for Contemplation)

Follow the same process as in the previous chapters, keeping your pen nearby.

1. In your current relationship, have you spent more time and energy on research or development? What areas need more development—expectation, interrogation, observation, investigation or preparation, desperation, stimulation, and celebration?

2. How much preparation did you and your significant other put into your relationship? In what areas would more preparation have prevented current problems or alleviated issues? What advice would *you* give to someone wanting to prepare for a serious relationship?

"You"

With 0 meaning "none" and 3 meaning "an amount that reflects thoroughness," write a number for each question below.

How much research and development do I put into the decisions I make? _____

How much research and development do I put into the decisions with life-long ripples such as my relationships? _____

Have I conducted adequate research into verifying the character of my beloved to make sure that he is who he says he is? _____

Have I spent enough time conducting the little tests of compatibility that are essential if I am to commit and spend a lifetime with this person? _____

How much insight have I developed from my research? _____

Any score below 12 indicates you need to beef up your research skills.

"Do" a Search

In our age of nanotechnology you have access to more information than our grandparents ever dreamed of having. Find out all you can about your prospective partner's past, present, and future. Use this list to make sure you take advantage of all the resources available.

Checklist for research.
Ask those who know your prospective partner from . . .

_____ high school

_____ college

_____ their old neighborhood

_____ work (current and past jobs)

_____ church (current and past)

Do Internet research by . . .

_____ a "Google" search

_____ checking other helpful sites

What do you know for sure?

List what you learn. You may find yourself tempted to list things you think or feel about this person, but stick with the facts—information that you've verified in some way or had verified through another person.

Facts I know   How I know this fact*

_____   _____

_____   _____

_____   _____

_____   _____

_____   _____

_____   _____

_____   _____

_____   _____

_____   _____

_____   _____

*Firsthand observation, his mother told you, a mutual friend shared the detail.

After you've spent a few minutes listing the facts, think about what's missing—what you don't know about this person that you wish you did.

Make a list of at least ten questions that you need to ask this person in order to grow in the relationship. Some of them may overlap with the questions in this book but try to make them as specific to your relationship as possible. And then set aside some time to ask them.

1. _____   _____

2. _____   _____

3. _____   _____

4. _____   _____

5. _____   _____

6. _____   _____

7. _____   _____

8. _____   _____

9. _____   _____

10. _____   _____

nine
Be Interested and Interesting
Keeping Your Relationship Fresh

> *Before you begin this portion of the* Making Great Decisions Workbook, *read Chapter Nine, "Before You Commit—Development" (pages 135–144), in* Making Great Decisions *(formerly titled* Before You Do*).*

A fter you've gathered data, gotten answers to your questions, and reached some measure of understanding of who the other person really is, then you are ready to implement the next phase of your relationship assessment—the development of what it will take for you as a couple to make it for the long haul.

"Before" (Questions for Contemplation)

Follow the same process as in the previous chapters, your pen handy.

1. Which questions have you already asked your date or spouse and had answered? Which ones still need to be asked?

2. Which of these questions do you regard as the most difficult to ask? The most embarrassing?

3. Which of these questions have you answered for your significant other? Did you volunteer information for some or did the other person have to ask in each case? What does this reveal about your style of communication?

4. What questions are not on this list that you believe must be answered before you marry someone?

5. What have you recently discovered about your significant other that you wish you had known sooner? What prevented your knowing this sooner?

"You"—Learning to Listen to Our Instincts

What's the most desperate you've ever been with another person?

_____

_____

If you find yourself staring blankly at that fill-in line consider these "True" or "False" statements:

I have found myself feeling desperate in a relationship.

I have found myself feeling emotionally not my best self in a relationship.

I would think about my beloved constantly.

I would wonder where they were.

I would wonder what they are doing.

I would wonder when I would see them again.

I ceased to have an existence of my own.

I stopped calling my friends.

I dropped everything to run to their side whenever they called.

When my partner was happy, I was happy.

When my partner was miserable, I was miserable.

I had no identity of my own.

My entire existence was wrapped up in my relationship.

Nothing else in my life mattered but that relationship.

I just enjoyed having someone who seemed to want me.

How desperate has your current partner been with you?

_____

_____

If you find yourself staring blankly at that fill-in line consider these "True" or "False" statements about your partner:

has no interests or life of their own

calls day and night

makes me the center of their life 24/7

has holes in the psyche or existence that they are looking to me to fill

What red flags have you ignored in the past?

_____

_____

What has been the consequence of ignoring your instincts?

_____

_____

"Do"—Your interests outside the relationship

We must maintain a sense of who we are in life outside of our relationship so that we can bring our whole self to the table when partnering up. Consider and write down . . .

interests I had before this relationship _____

friends I had before this relationship _____

hobbies I had before this relationship _____

activities I had before this relationship _____

Plan to put aside time each week specifically to return to these people, activities, and interests.

Week 1 _____

Week 2 _____

Week 3 _____

Week 4 _____

Week 5 _____

Interesting conversation

In order to keep your relationship moving forward, you and your partner must find ways to keep emotionally or intellectually stimulated.

What's the most stimulating discussion you and your partner have ever had with one another?

_____

_____

_____

_____

What makes it memorable?

_____

_____

_____

_____

How often do you feel stimulated by this person?

_____

_____

_____

_____

What interests do you share?

_____

_____

_____

_____

While activities outside the relationship are important, so are activities that the two of you can do together. Consider these to spark interesting and lively conversations. Give yourself fifteen points for each one you try and twenty-five points for each one that you both feel resulted in a dynamic conversation. Aim for a hundred points each month!

1. Attend a lecture or seminar together on a topic you are both interested in. Go out for a cup of coffee after and discuss what you heard.

2. Read the same book. Talk about it over dinner.

3. Get the Sunday paper and share a favorite story from your favorite section.

4. Go out to see or rent an interesting documentary or movie and talk about what you saw.

5. Invite some interesting friends out to dinner or to a party. Discuss current events or community issues.

6. Take up a sport that you can enjoy together.

7. Take up a hobby that you can enjoy together.

Score: _____

Celebrating each other

Feeling celebrated in a love relationship is essential to its health. It's nice to be the object of the celebration and it's equally important to plan celebrations for your partner.

How does your current love celebrate you?

_____

_____

_____

_____

How often do you feel celebrated? Only on special occasions or more often than that?

_____

_____

_____

_____

How often do you celebrate your partner?

_____

_____

_____

_____

Plan to do something to celebrate your partner, expecting nothing in return. Here are a few ideas. Again, give yourself fifteen points for each one you try and twenty-five points for each one that you both feel resulted in a dynamic conversation. Aim for a hundred points each month!

1. Cook a nice dinner made up of your partner's favorite foods. Set the table, bring out the good china and linens. Light some candles and dress the table with flowers. Turn off the cell phone and the pagers and the BlackBerrys and just be together. Maybe there's a recent accomplishment to celebrate, or maybe you are just celebrating being in love. You get to choose.

2. Do something unexpected. Buy him the latest CD of his favorite artist and leave it for him on the seat of his car. Get those pictures from her camera of your last vacation developed and surprise her with a photo album already organized and labeled.

3. Run a nice bath or give him or her a nice foot or hand massage after a long day.

4. Write him a note telling him how special he is, and leave it in his coat pocket or briefcase.

5. Pick up the laundry, dry cleaning, or unload the dishwasher so she doesn't have to.

6. Make a date night. Every week put aside time where it's just the two of you. No matter what, you commit to this time together and schedule nothing else. And don't just sit at home and fall asleep in front of the TV. Plan something special that's about just celebrating the two of you. It doesn't have to be expensive; it can be something as simple as going for a walk, driving to the beach to watch the sunset, or listening to a free outdoor concert. Just making the time to celebrate how important you are to each other is what matters most.

ten

Before You Get Engaged
Twenty Final Exam Questions

This part of the workbook is designed to accommodate your answers to the questions in Chapter Ten, "Before You Get Engaged—Twenty Final Exam Questions You Must Ask" (pages 145–162), in Making Great Decisions (formerly titled Before You Do).

These questions are what I consider to be the twenty most important questions to ask before you decide to get engaged. Answer these questions together with your partner.

1. What do you expect?

_____

_____

_____

_____

1. What do you expect?

_____

_____

_____

_____

2. What are your most prized possessions?

_____

_____

_____

_____

3. Where do you stand on faith?

_____

_____

_____

4. What was your last major relationship like? How did it end?

_____

_____

_____

2. What are your most prized possessions?

3. Where do you stand on faith?

4. What was your last major relationship like? How did it end?

5. What are your ideas about sexuality?

_____

_____

_____

_____

6. Do you know your HIV/AIDS status?

_____

_____

_____

7. What are the secrets that you keep? Will you trust me to keep them too?

_____

_____

_____

5. What are your ideas about sexuality?

6. Do you know your HIV/AIDS status?

7. What are the secrets that you keep? Will you trust me to keep them too?

8. Have you ever been arrested and
do you have a criminal record?

_____

_____

_____

_____

8. Have you ever been arrested and
do you have a criminal record?

_____

_____

_____

_____

9. Do you have children or "other"
children outside marriage?

_____

_____

_____

_____

9. Do you have children or "other"
children outside marriage?

_____

_____

_____

_____

10. How do you feel about having
children?

_____

_____

_____

10. How do you feel about having
children?

_____

_____

_____

11. How do you feel about disciplin-
ing children?

_____

_____

_____

_____

12. What are the roles of a husband
and a wife for you?

_____

_____

_____

_____

13. What role do you see your parents, siblings, and extended family
playing in our relationship?

_____

_____

_____

11. How do you feel about disciplin-
ing children?

_____

_____

_____

_____

12. What are the roles of a husband
and a wife for you?

_____

_____

_____

_____

13. What role do you see your parents, siblings, and extended family
playing in our relationship?

_____

_____

_____

14. How do you handle disagreements and disappointments?

_____

_____

_____

_____

15. What is your vision for this family?
Where would you like us to be in ten
years or twenty?

_____

_____

_____

16. How satisfied are you with your
present career?

_____

_____

_____

14. How do you handle disagreements and disappointments?

15. What is your vision for this family?
Where would you like us to be in ten
years or twenty?

16. How satisfied are you with your
present career?

17. What is your debt-to-income ratio?

Housing debts
    mortgage expense _____
    home insurance _____
    taxes _____

        Subtotal + _____

Other recurring debts
    student loans _____
    car loans _____
    child support
      payments _____
    credit card
      payments _____

        Subtotal + _____

        Total debt = _____

        Divided by gross
        monthly income _____

        Debt-to-income
        ratio _____

18. Is there any need or desire for a prenuptial agreement?

_____

_____

_____

---

17. What is your debt-to-income ratio?

Housing debts
    mortgage expense _____
    home insurance _____
    taxes _____

        Subtotal + _____

Other recurring debts
    student loans _____
    car loans _____
    child support
      payments _____
    credit card
      payments _____

        Subtotal + _____

        Total debt = _____

        Divided by gross
        monthly income _____

        Debt-to-income
        ratio _____

18. Is there any need or desire for a prenuptial agreement?

_____

_____

_____

19. Do you have a will or a living
will, and can we talk about it?

_____

_____

_____

_____

19. Do you have a will or a living
will, and can we talk about it?

_____

_____

_____

_____

20. What annoys you the most about
me? What do you enjoy most about
being with me?

_____

_____

_____

_____

20. What annoys you the most about
me? What do you enjoy most about
being with me?

_____

_____

_____

_____

eleven
Marrying Well

Before you begin this portion of the Making Great Decisions Workbook, *read Chapter Eleven, "Before You Marry" (pages 163–177), in* Making Great Decisions *(formerly titled* Before You Do*).*

It can be challenging to stay in a committed relationship. This section is to help free your relationship from the shackles of false expectations and limited perspectives.

"Before" (Questions for Contemplation)

Follow the same contemplation process as in the beginning chapters of this workbook, keeping your pen nearby, but not writing down anything until you've spent time thinking about all the questions.

1. In what ways are you and your partner opposites?

2. How have you handled the resulting tensions when you disagree? What's been the most challenging area of disagreement? Why?

3. What one attitude or belief would you change about your partner if you could? Why? What do you think he or she would want to change about you? Why?

4. In what ways have you changed your expectations about what marriage requires? In what areas do you need to allow more flexibility?

"You" _____

I am the opposite of my partner in these three fun/interesting ways:

_____

_____

_____

I am the opposite of my partner in these three important ways:

_____

_____

_____

The last time we disagreed, I . . .

did _____

_____

said _____

felt _____

During the most important disagreement we have had, I . . .

did _____

said _____

felt _____

The last time we disagreed, my partner . . .

did _____

said _____

_____

felt _____

_____

During the most important disagreement we have had, my partner . . .

did _____

_____

said _____

_____

felt _____

_____

We have agreed to handle the resulting tensions when we disagree by . . .

_____

_____

_____

_____

Our most challenging area of disagreement is . . .

_____

_____

_____

_____

The one attitude or belief I would change about my partner, if I could, is . . .

_____

_____

_____

_____

The one attitude or belief my partner would change about me probably is . . .

_____

_____

_____

_____

The area of flexibility my partner probably feels I need is . . .

_____

_____

_____

_____

Since meeting my partner, I have changed these expectations about what marriage requires:

_____

_____

_____

_____

"Do"—Give Unconditional Love

The voyage toward ultimate fulfillment occurs every day as you find your rhythm together. Before you marry, discuss the diversity of views, cultures, families, and opinions that are combining. Listen, liberate, and lavish the other person with the freedom of unconditional love.

Gather photo albums, pictures, and a family tree of your family if anyone has constructed one, and ask your mate to do the same. Create a scrapbook.

His family traditions

_____

_____

_____

_____

_____

Her family traditions

_____

_____

_____

_____

_____

Create a family tree for each of you with the following people.

Father	_____	Father	_____
Mother	_____	Mother	_____
Stepfather	_____	Stepfather	_____
Stepmother	_____	Stepmother	_____
Siblings	_____	Siblings	_____
Grandfather	_____	Grandfather	_____
Grandmother	_____	Grandmother	_____
Aunts	_____	Aunts	_____
Uncles	_____	Uncles	_____

This exercise will do much to enlighten the two of you about the traditions from which you both come and will go a long way to shedding light on your behaviors and some of the things that are important to you.

Do fight fair

Disagreements happen in every relationship. How you disagree goes a long way to determining the success or failure of your relationship. Ask yourself the following questions about when you fight and answer "True" or "False."

I express my feelings in a constructive way, remaining calm and rational.

My goal is to not be right, but to reach a mutually beneficial solution.

My goal is not to get revenge but to restore the relationship.

My goal is not to get the last word but to listen and understand and also be understood.

I keep our disagreements private.

I avoid sharing our disagreements with the neighbors, friends, our children, and our families.

I keep my discussion in the present and refrain from bringing up old disagreements.

I focus on the issue at hand and never name-call or attack my partner personally.

I work hard to keep my voice calm and de-emotionalize the disagreement.

I keep a goal in mind so I know when the discussion is over.

I pick my battles and do not make a federal case out of every little thing.

If I see the disagreement escalating to a heated argument, I work at defusing the emotion.

When my partner does not fight fair, I do not take that as license for me to fight unfairly.

If you answered "False" to any of these statements, you are not fighting fair. A willingness to be flexible and release the need to be right and to win will go a long way to a more stable, long-lasting relationship.

Do forgive

We all make mistakes. Perfection only exists in God our savior. Recall Jesus' words "Father, forgive them; for they know not what they do" (Luke 23:34, KJV). Offering the forgiveness you wish to receive is a good way to ensure that your relationship remains healthy and free of the disease of bitterness.
     Ask yourself the following questions:

What needs forgiving in our relationship?

What has kept me from asking for forgiveness?

What has kept me from granting forgiveness?

If you find that you are holding on to feelings of unforgiveness, consider these activities to help you move on.

Write out your grievance.

I am angry with _____ because he/she _____.

It made me feel _____

And I don't feel I can forgive him/her because _____

_____

_____

Now consider the reason you can't forgive: is it because the person really did something so awful that they don't deserve forgiveness, or is it because your feelings are hurt? If it is the latter, consider calling or sitting down with your loved one to discuss it. Don't recount to family and friends what they did wrong; go to the source—it's the only way to truly heal a situation.

Make a list of the people you've hurt who have not forgiven you.

_____

_____

_____

_____

Recall how bad you felt when they didn't forgive you.

_____

_____

_____

_____

_____

Make a list of the people you've hurt who *have* forgiven you.

_____

_____

_____

_____

Recall the feeling of relief you experienced whey they did. Wouldn't you like to extend that feeling to your loved one, who is probably feeling pretty bad for hurting you?

_____

_____

_____

_____

Is there someone you need to call to ask for forgiveness?

_____

_____

_____

_____

_____

Pray. Ask God to help you find the strength to forgive. And pray for the person who you need to forgive. Write your prayer here.

_____

_____

_____

_____

_____

Demonstrate you are over it, by doing something tangible. List things you can do that would show you have extended forgiveness.

Make or give them a gift.

Take them out for a nice meal.

Make them dinner.

Send them a card.

_____

_____

_____

_____

Be patient. Forgiveness sometimes takes time. But keep working at it every day and you will soon experience the relief that comes with letting go.

twelve
Risk It All
Learning to Step Out on Faith

> *Before you begin this portion of the* Making Great Decisions Workbook, *read Chapter Twelve, "Before You Decide to Take a Risk for Your Marriage" (pages 179–189), in* Making Great Decisions *(formerly titled* Before You Do*).*

We all face new experiences with some degree of angst. This section is to help you feel the fear and do it anyway.

"Before" (Questions for Contemplation)

Follow the same process as in the previous chapters, with your pen handy.

1. When is the last time you felt nervous before you tried something new?

2. How did you handle it?

3. Did you feel prepared and ready for the new experience? Or were you just thrown into the water and left to swim?

4. How do you prepare for experiences that you know will make you nervous, such as pubic speaking, performing, meeting a new person, etc.?

5. Have you ever let nerves keep you from trying something new? How did you later feel about doing that?

"You"

Admitting you feel fear is the first step toward handling it. Circle the words you tend to use instead of the word "fear."

Terror	Horror	Panic
Dread	Fright	Alarm
Trepidation	Anxiety	Scared
Apprehension	Nightmare	Fright
Worry	Phobia	
Concern	Afraid	

I let fear keep me from . . .

_____

_____

_____

Later I felt _____ about doing that.

List the three things you are most afraid of in relationships:

_____

_____

_____

"Do"—Handle Fear

Fear is a natural and normal emotion and a part of life. It could be a signal of danger. But fear can also just be a sign that we are stepping out and living on the edge of territory we have yet to explore. How you handle fear can mean the difference between performing at your best and shrinking under the pressure. One way to alleviate fear pangs is to be as *prepared* as possible for whatever it is you are about to do.

Complete each action word or phrase below with something you can do to address one of your three fears above.

Arrange _____

Coach _____

Get ready _____

Groom _____

Make ready _____

Organize _____

Plan _____

Practice _____

Prime _____

Put in order _____

Set up _____

Train _____

Warm up _____

Visualize Your Success

Visualizing yourself achieving success is another way to alleviate fear.

Close your eyes and sit still. Picture yourself at the top of a long staircase. And each stair is numbered, starting at one hundred. See yourself stepping down stair by stair, and as you descend count back from one hundred, ninety-nine, ninety-eight, ninety-seven, ninety-six . . . count all the way down to one.

When you get to one, see yourself walking through a large wooden door. Push on it, and it will open to a beautiful place—somewhere you love and feel totally safe and comfortable. In the corner are a group of people who you just love, who support you unconditionally no matter what. They are smiling and waving and glad to see you. Walk over to them, let them embrace you, listen to their words of encouragement, and thank them for being there.

Now turn away and walk to the center of the room Stand for a moment, taking in the love and positive energy in the room.

Now picture yourself doing the thing that scares you. Whatever it is, picture yourself doing it; and whatever success means to you, see that happening. Imagine the sights, the smells, the sounds that would accompany this accomplishment. Think about how you would feel if all went well. Look back at your supporters: they are still there, smiling, clapping, and cheering. Now, you've done it!

Use this page to write down what you just visualized. Be sure to include . . .

the beautiful safe place that you love.

the smiling, waving people you love, who support you unconditionally.

their words of encouragement.

the love and positive energy in the room.

the thing that scares you.

what success means to you—the sights, smells, sounds of accomplishment.

your feelings of all going well.

Now, it's just a matter of faith. Faith in your preparation, your ability, and most of all, in God to support you in whatever it is you wish to do. Go for it!

thirteen
Choosing How and Where to Live

> *Before you begin this portion of the* Making Great Decisions Workbook, *read Chapter Thirteen, "Before You Buy a House" (pages 191–204), in* Making Great Decisions *(formerly titled* Before You Do*).*

One of the greatest experiences that any couple can share together is creating a home. The choice of a home is an important relationship decision. This section will help you make it wisely.

"Before" (Questions for Contemplation)

Follow the same process as the previous chapters, with your pen handy.

1. What experiences have you had with buying a home? If you have purchased a home before, what will you do differently the next time? If you have not bought a house before, what has prevented your purchase?

2. When faced with buying a house, are you more likely to make a logical decision or an emotional one? How can you find a balance between the two?

3. What resources have you consulted so far in your consideration of buying a house—Internet, friends, family, newspaper, real estate agent? What has proved most helpful? Why?

4. If you were going to move today but remain in the same area, where would you move? Why would you want to live there? What homes are available in that area? What keeps you from looking in that vicinity?

5. How satisfied are you with your present home? How well does it meet the needs of you and your family? What would you change about it to make it more suitable?

"You"

Free-associate the term "home ownership," noting all the words that it brings to mind. Do your best to connect your feelings to words.

_____   _____   _____

_____   _____   _____

_____   _____   _____

_____   _____   _____

Now circle the words that are positive.

List here the words that are negative:

_____

_____

_____

Use each negative word in a sentence beginning with "I":

_____

_____

_____

Examine your "I" sentences. Are they realistic, factual? Or, are they feelings?

Place an *F* for fact, next to each sentence that is factual and an *E* next to next to each sentence that is emotional. Emotions are just as valid as facts. Talk over your sentences with your partner or someone else you trust.

Turn back to page 6, to your list of true values. Consider how purchasing a home achieves or does not line up with your values.

Value   How home ownership exhibits value

_____   _____

_____   _____

_____   _____

_____   _____

_____   _____

_____   _____

_____   _____

"Do" _____

Worksheet for people thinking about buying a home

Step 1: Find a mortgage that's right for you.
The most common types are thirty-year and fifteen-year fixed mortgages where the interest rate is fixed for the term of the loan. Other types include adjustable-rate mortgages, called ARMs, where the interest can vary over time; hybrid ARMs; jumbos; assumables; and seller financing.

How long do I want the tax benefit of mortgage payments? _____

How long do I want the serious obligation of mortgage payments? _____

Step 2: Determine how much house you can afford.

Considerations:

Amount I can put down: _____

Monthly payments I can manage: _____

Real estate taxes I can manage: _____

Closing costs: _____

Insurance (home owners): _____

Insurance (private mortgage insurance if I put less than 20 percent down):

_____

Existing monthly payments on debt obligations including credit cards, alimony, and student loans (should not be more than 36 percent of your pretax income):

_____

_____

_____

Step 3: Check your credit.

My three credit scores:

_____

_____

_____

Errors and problems to clear up:

_____

_____

_____

Step 4: Prequalification and preapproval.
"Prequalified" means that a lender will review your financial history before you find a home. "Preapproved" means that a lender will check your credit

and provide you with a letter stating that you've been preapproved for a certain amount. Both of these will help improve your purchasing power.

Prequalification_____

Preapproval _____

Step 5: Gather the necessary paperwork.
- Tax documents
- Pay stubs showing yearly income
- Social Security numbers

Step 6: Find a lender.
Check the rates and lenders on Bankrate.com. Remember that just because a loan has the lowest rate doesn't mean it's the best one for you. In addition to the rate, check on points (prepaid mortgage interest that will increase your up-front costs), APR, and other fees associated with a particular loan.

Mortgage Comparison

Lender #1   Lender #2   Lender #3

_____   _____   _____

_____   _____   _____

_____   _____   _____

Step 7: Assess your potential home.
An appraisal is part of the mortgage process and will ensure that you're paying the appropriate price for your home.

Appraisal: _____

Step 8: Prepare for closing.

Make sure the closing is scheduled before your loan commitment and any lock-in rate will expire. And be sure there is enough time to finish any loan documentation and complete any home inspections or repairs.

Closing date: _____

Step 9: Closing day!

At the closing you will have to sign legal documents and pay closing costs.
    Cashier's checks I will need for closing costs:

Surveying _____

Taxes _____

Insurance _____

Attorney fees _____

Agent fees _____

Points _____

Loan origination fees _____

PMI _____

Balance of down payment _____

Step 10: Servicing the mortgage.

At the closing, your mortgage lender must tell you who will be servicing your mortgage loan (to whom and where you will make payments). Traditionally, the mortgage banker would service the loan for the life of the mortgage on behalf of the investor. However, the servicing may be handled by a third party.

Monthly payments _____

To whom I will make payments _____

Address where I will send payments _____

List friends and family members who have purchased homes:

_____

_____

_____

_____

_____

Interview them about their experiences—ask what mistakes they made and what they've learned, so that you can avoid the same fate.

_____

_____

_____

_____

_____

_____

Recommended real estate agents:

_____

_____

_____

_____

_____

Recommended bankers or mortgage brokers:

_____

_____

_____

_____

_____

Other professionals recommended:

_____

_____

_____

_____

_____

_____

List friends and family members you respect, who live well, and are financially secure, but who rent:

_____

_____

_____

_____

_____

Interview them about their experiences and reasons for *not* purchasing their home. Compile the information you gather into these two lists:

Good reasons to own home now   Good reasons not to own home now

_____   _____

_____   _____

_____   _____

_____   _____

_____   _____

Circle the item most important to you—based on *both* the facts and your emotions!

fourteen

Deciding on the World's Most Important Job
Becoming a Parent

> *Before you begin this portion of the* Making Great Decisions Workbook, *read Chapter Fourteen, "Before You Have Children" (pages 205–219), in* Making Great Decisions *(formerly titled* Before You Do*).*

Children can teach us so much about ourselves, about God, and about the world around us. In addition to the crucial ways we invest in their lives, they also have an amazing influence on our own lives. The decision to have children is often a decision not made, however. The considerations in this chapter are just as important in hindsight as in foresight.

"Before" (Questions for Contemplation)

Follow the same process as in the previous chapters, with your pen handy.

1. How are children presently involved in your life? Do you already have children of your own or are you considering becoming parents for the first time? What has motivated or is motivating you to have children?

2. How has your experience with your parents influenced your view of parenting children of your own? Would your parenting style be similar to what you experienced or radically different? Why?

3. In your estimation, what are the most dangerous influences on children today? What are the results that you have experienced firsthand?

4. Regardless of whether you are presently a parent, how can you make a contribution to influence kids positively?

5. What's the hardest part of being a parent? Why?

"You"—Your Motivations for Becoming a Parent

Make sure your desires in are in line with your partner's regarding having children. You need to have these discussions before you need the home pregnancy test! Check all that apply.

Him: I want to become a parent to . . .

achieve status equal to my partner's previous liaison (which resulted in a child).

be financially supported.

build a family unit.

carry on my family name or my heritage.

create a lasting bond with someone.

feel like a real man.

give love to someone.

give purpose to my life.

have a permanent bond with the child's other parent.

have someone to love me.

keep me young.

please my partner.

support another being into a mature, well-rounded adult

Her: I want to become a parent to . . .

achieve status equal to my partner's previous liaison (which resulted in a child).

be financially supported.

build a family unit.

carry on my family name or my heritage.

create a lasting bond with someone.

feel like a complete woman.

give love to someone.

give purpose to my life.

have a permanent bond with the child's other parent.

have someone to love me.

keep me young.

please my partner.

support another being into a mature, well-rounded adult.

If either of you has checked any item other than the last one, I recommend some serious soul-searching before proceeding down the road to becoming a parent.

Consider your motivations for having children and ask your partner to do the same. Now each sit down with this list and write out your answers. Once you have both completed it, compare your answers. If they are similar, then you are likely to agree on the fundamentals regarding having children, but if they are very different, you might want to give the idea of having a baby some serious reconsideration.

Question	Think About	Your Answer	Your Partner's Answer
Why do you want a child?	There is a difference between wanting a child and feeling that you need a child. Children are not meant to fix a marriage, give you comfort, or fill a hole in your life.		

Question	Think About	Your Answer	Your Partner's Answer
Do you understand that having a child is a lifelong commitment?	Everyone thinks little babies are cute. But eventually they turn into teenagers and sometimes into adults who can't manage to leave the nest.		
Are you ready to stop focusing on yourself?	Having a child means things will change forever going forward. And the world will no longer revolve around you. Are you ready for that?		
Do you and your partner have different feelings about having a baby?	You may be ready to have a baby but your partner may not be. Having a child must be a mutual decision between partners. How do you feel about waiting if your partner is not ready?		
How would you feel if your partner decided that he or she *never* wanted children?			

These are just suggested questions that will get the discussions about having children started. Be sure you are both on the same page before you take the life-changing step of having a child, both for your sake and your future child's.

"Do"—Understand Child Rearing

Mark the statements below "True" or "False."

_____ The act of nurturing a family will be the most rewarding task I will ever undertake.

_____ The act of nurturing a family will be the most difficult task I will ever undertake.

_____ The act of nurturing a family will be the most dynamic task I will ever undertake.

_____ God meant for everyone to be a parent.

_____ Children today do just as well in single-parent households because that is the norm.

The first three are true. The last two are patently false!

Spend some time with a child this week. If you already have a child of your own, then make extra time and visit a park, museum, zoo, or other fun location you know the child will enjoy. If you don't have a child of your own, consider spending time with a niece or nephew or friend's child. Or perhaps volunteer at a children's organization or school. Journal your experience in the space below.

How did you communicate with the child?

_____

_____

_____

How do you think you come across to this child? Circle the words that apply and add your own.

protective

instructive

humorous

stern

curious

_____

_____

_____

_____

fifteen
When Leaving Is the Only Answer

> *Before you begin this portion of the* Making Great Decisions *Workbook, read Chapter Fifteen, "Before You Divorce" (pages 221–237), in* Making Great Decisions *(formerly titled* Before You Do*).*

This book is about how to divorce-proof your marriage by making great decisions. However, divorce is a reality, and here's what you must consider before you sever the bond.

"Before" (Questions for Contemplation)

Follow the same process as in the previous chapters, with your pen handy.

1. What impact has divorce—perhaps that of your parents, siblings, friends, your own—had on your life? How has this impact shaped the way you view your commitment to your spouse or boyfriend/girlfriend?

2. How often do you or your partner throw around the d-word? Under what circumstances? Do you regard this as a casual threat in the heat of an argument or something that either of you would seriously consider?

3. What has been the most difficult offense for which you have forgiven your partner? For which he or she has forgiven you? What impact have this offense and subsequent forgiveness had on your commitment to each other?

4. When have you been tempted to relate in an inappropriate way with someone outside your marriage or relationship? How did you respond to this temptation? What did you learn about yourself? About your marriage or relationship?

5. How often do you currently think about divorce in your present relationship? Does your partner know how often you consider it?

"You"—What Is Your Deal Breaker?

We all have lines in the sand, and it is important for you each to know your loved one's line. What's considered an inappropriate relationship to you might seem natural to your partner. Before you marry, understand what offenses you believe you won't be able to forgive.

Make a list of five offenses for which you could envision yourself getting divorced. Write them down and share them with your partner. This way you will both enter into marriage with an understanding of what you each expect in terms of behavior and relationships with others.

My Deal Breakers   My Partner's Deal Breakers

1. _____   _____

2. _____   _____

3. _____   _____

4. _____   _____

5. _____   _____

List those close to you who have divorced—perhaps your parents, siblings, friends, or even you.

Name	The impact this divorce had on your life					
	Great	4	3	2	1	Nothing
	Great	4	3	2	1	Nothing
	Great	4	3	2	1	Nothing
	Great	4	3	2	1	Nothing
	Great	4	3	2	1	Nothing
	Great	4	3	2	1	Nothing

The d-word

Perhaps you or your partner take the idea of divorce casually. Maybe divorce is so common in your family or community that you are desensitized to its impact. To practice the power of a commitment to stay together, fill in the blank next to each word below with its opposite:

Annul   _____

Break up   _____

Detach   _____

Disconnect   _____

Dissociate   _____

Distance   _____

Separate   _____

Split   _____

If you find this a tough exercise, it's because our society has conditioned us for divorce rather than lifelong commitment!

"Do"—Trust

One of the quickest ways to undermine a relationship is to keep secrets from your partner or spouse. Trust is the cornerstone to any relationship.

List any secrets you are presently keeping from your spouse or significant other.

_____

_____

_____

A secret may be a heavy burden such as an affair, inappropriate emotional attachment, or addiction, or it may be something more subtle such as being resentful about missing date night, always putting his or her work first, or not keeping promises.

How would your partner feel if you shared your secrets?

_____

_____

_____

_____

_____

Before you rush to confess them, consider their impact on this person you love and the relationship you are building. You might consider seeking the counsel of someone you trust. Always consider if you are sharing something because it will make you feel better to get something off your chest or if it is something your partner will want to know. Use the script formatting provided below to project what the confessional conversation between you two would be like. Write the dialogue you imagine.

You:

_____

_____

_____

Your partner:

_____

_____

_____

You:

_____

_____

_____

Your partner:

_____

_____

_____

You:

_____

_____

_____

Your partner:

_____

_____

_____

You:

_____

_____

_____

Your partner:

_____

_____

_____

You:

_____

_____

_____

Your partner:

_____

_____

_____

Pray for discernment about what to share and what to keep to yourself. Write your prayer in the space below.

_____

_____

_____

_____

_____

_____

_____

_____

_____

sixteen

Staying in Touch with Your Dreams

Before you begin this portion of the Making Great Decisions Workbook, *read Chapter Sixteen, "Before You Settle for Less" (pages 239–249), in* Making Great Decisions *(formerly titled* Before You Do*).*

M any men and women reach a certain plateau in their lives where it feels like the best of their lives is behind them. They no longer feel they can do anything in the world. No matter where you are in life, you need not feel that way. This section is to help you, as Langston Hughes wrote, "Hold fast to dreams . . ."

"Before" (Questions for contemplation)

Follow the same process as in the previous chapters, with your pen handy.

1. As you reflect on your life, do you think of yourself as a quitter? Why or why not? What do you associate with quitting?

2. When have you been tempted to quit in your life? Regardless of whether you did, what were the consequences? When do you wish you had quit something sooner?

3. What's the most important dream in your life on which you have given up? What caused you to give it up? How often do you think about it presently?

4. Who has had the most positive influence on you in terms of encouraging you to persevere? How has their support and example helped you continue?

5. What's the greatest risk you've ever taken? What did you learn from it? Would you do it again? Why or why not?

"You"

Which of the following have you done? Note the circumstance and how you felt about it.

	Circumstance	My feelings
Given up	_____	_____
Left	_____	_____
Resigned	_____	_____
Walked out	_____	_____
Abandoned	_____	_____
Given notice	_____	_____
Deserted	_____	_____

	Circumstance	My feelings
Persevered	_____	_____
Persisted	_____	_____
Continued	_____	_____
Kept at it	_____	_____
Stuck with it	_____	_____
Remained	_____	_____

Giving up on dreams is like giving up on hope. Hope and dreams are all we really have. Sure, some dreams are not meant to come true. Yet many of the dreams we give up on can be resurrected with a little love and care. Life is not always good, but it is good enough.

Before you quit your dream, consider these "True or False" questions:

_____ If nothing changed from this point forward, I am satisfied with my life.

_____ I have sometimes quit my dreams prematurely.

_____ Reassessing, readjusting, my dream to better suit my circumstances could work.

_____ I need new dreams for the person I am now.

_____ If I want to start a business, take a trip, or begin a second career, it is possible.

"Do"—Mine for Dreams

1. Sign up for a local seminar, conference, or workshop.

2. Join a group. If you like to paint, join an art group. If you like to write, sign up for a writing class or join a writers' group. If you like to sing, take singing lessons. If you like to cook, take a cooking class. Immerse yourself in the topic of your dreams for a few weeks—even if it's just an hour a week.

3. Spend a day at the library or in the bookstore. Find everything you can about your dream by spending the day at the library doing research. Read everything you can find. Do Internet searches on your desired area. There is a magazine for every interest. Find one that specializes in what you want to pursue and get a subscription.

4. Go back to school. Sure, it requires a time commitment. And we are already highly squeezed for extra time. But once you decide you really want to pursue a dream, additional education may be required. Start slowly with one or two courses. And if you are married, ask for support at home. You don't have to do it all on your own. And when your family sees how happy it makes you to pursue something that makes your heart sing, they are likely going to be happy to pitch in.

You will notice your spirit start to come alive after just one class or group or research foray. Journal your experience of the first class. Be sure to write about . . .

the place

the people

the work you did

energy in the room

your feelings

How could the class expose you to ways and people who can help you make your dream become a reality?

Set up informational meetings

One of the best ways to get information about pursuing a dream is to call someone who already does what you want to do. If you don't know anyone personally, ask friends and family if they know someone or look up people in the phone book or online. Send them an e-mail or a letter introducing yourself. Tell them you'll only take twenty minutes of their time but that you'd like to buy them a cup of coffee or tea and pick their brain about what they do. Be prepared. Do your research. Have questions ready to ask. Here are a few ideas:

1. Why do you do what you do?

2. What do you like best about it?

3. What are the challenges?

4. Does it require a certain amount of education? Special degrees? Other training?

5. What's the best way to get started doing what you do?

6. May I call you from time to time for further information?

7. Is there someone else you could recommend that I speak to?

It's not what you know, but who you know

Devise a new plan and assign dates to your endeavors.

Dream Plan

I _____ (fill in your name) want to pursue

_____

By _____ (date) _____ I will have talked to
three people who do what I want to do.

By _____ (date) _____ I will have read
the following book or signed up for the following seminar or class:

_____

Start small. Start out by taking a small risk at least once a week that will move
you closer to your goal. Write each risk into your plan and assign it a date.
And then be sure you complete it by the date or reschedule it as necessary.
(Be careful to not get into the habit of rescheduling so much that you never
accomplish anything.)

Surround yourself with like-minded, positive people for support. Make
a list of people who you admire for stepping out in their own lives, who take
risks, and who understand what pursuing dreams is all about.

_____   _____

_____   _____

_____   _____

_____   _____

Start by taking a risk, a small one at first, some little step toward realizing your goal. Then take another step, maybe a little bigger risk. Do it again and again, until each time the risks you take will get easier to deal with and soon you'll find yourself stronger, more courageous, and steps down the road toward where you want to be in your life, and closer to making your dreams come true.

A new look for your dream

You may be thinking: OK, my dream was to be a professional ball player, I am forty-five years old, and that will *never* happen no matter how I dream. Your new dream could be to be involved with the game of baseball. You could coach a Little League or high school team. You could work as a referee. You could get season tickets to your favorite team. You could go to a baseball clinic or join a local league for fun. You could volunteer at a baseball museum. Expand your thinking so that you can be exposed to what you want, maybe not in the way you planned, but remaining open to a new look for your dream.

Write your unrealized dream below and three options that could give your old dream a new look.

My old dream:

New look #1 _____

New look #2 _____

New look #3 _____

seventeen
Knowing When to Do Battle and How *Not* To

> *Before you begin this portion of the* Making Great Decisions Workbook, *read Chapter Seventeen, "Before You Fight" (pages 251–269), in* Making Great Decisions *(formerly titled* Before You Do*).*

If you have developed a defensive stance that prevents you from accepting what you need, here's help in discerning when to fight and when to let your defenses down.

"Before" (Questions for Contemplation)

Follow the same process as in the previous chapters, with your pen handy.

1. When faced with conflict, do you tend to fight more or take flight more? What has shaped this tendency in you? What past experiences have contributed to your inclination?

2. What fights do you need to relinquish in order to move on with your life? What are you protecting yourself from? Why?

3. Are there areas in your life where you should be fighting more? Have you become weary and given up on some fights that need to be resumed?

4. How often are you a peacemaker? Would others describe you as a good listener or a better talker? In what area of your life do you presently need to be the peacemaker?

5. Do you tend to jump to conclusions and become suspicious or defensive when offered help? Is there a present situation in your life that you have shunned and attempted to fight?

"You" _____

Conflicts
Various issues are listed on pages 178–179. In the column below, write each issue that most reflects your tendencies as they are now.

When faced with conflict,   When faced with conflict,
I tend to fight   I tend to take flight

_____   _____

_____   _____

_____   _____

_____   _____

_____   _____

_____   _____

_____   _____

_____   _____

Conflict with my partner

Conflict with my children

Conflict with my stepchild's natural parent

Conflict with my mother

Conflict with my father

Conflict with my sibling _____ (specify)

Conflict with my in-laws

Conflict with other family members _____ (specify)

Conflict with my boss

Conflict with my coworkers

Conflict with my subordinates at work

Conflict with my church leadership

Conflict with my church family

Conflict with my neighbors

Conflict with my friends _____ (specify)

Conflict when driving

Conflict in public situations

Conflict in groups/teams/organizations I belong to _____ (specify)

Conflict with those in authority

Conflict with God

Conflict with my conscience

Conflict in politics

Affirmations

Circle the statements below that apply to you. Take quiet time for several consecutive days to recite those you circle.

I am conscious of the areas in my life where I presently need to be the peacemaker.

I am conscious of the areas in my life where I should be fighting more.

I am conscious of the past experiences that contributed to my inclination to fight.

I am conscious of what I am protecting myself from.

I am conscious that there is a present situation in my life that I have shunned.

I am conscious that there is a present situation in my life that I have attempted to fight.

I am often a peacemaker.

I have become weary and given up on some fights that need to be resumed.

I know what shaped this tendency in me.

I tend to jump to conclusions and become suspicious or defensive when offered help.

After you've spent time reciting your chosen affirmations, fill in three issues for those that apply to you.

Areas in my life where I presently need to be the peacemaker:

1. _____

_____

2. _____

_____

3. _____

_____

Areas in my life where I should be fighting more:

1. _____

_____

2. _____

_____

3. _____

_____

Past experiences that contributed to my inclination:

1. _____

_____

2. _____

_____

3. _____

_____

I am protecting myself from:

1. _____

_____

2. _____

_____

3. _____

_____

Present situations in my life that I have shunned:

1. _____

_____

2. _____

_____

3. _____

_____

Present situations in my life that I have attempted to fight:

1. _____

_____

2. _____

_____

3. _____

_____

I need to make peace with:

1. _____

_____

2. _____

_____

3. _____

_____

I have become weary and given up on these fights that I need to resume:

1. _____

_____

2. _____

_____

3. _____

_____

This tendency in me was shaped by:

1. _____

_____

2. _____

_____

3. _____

_____

I wrongly jumped to conclusions about:

1. _____

_____

2. _____

_____

3. _____

_____

I wrongly became suspicious about:

1. _____

_____

2. _____

3. _____

_____

I wrongly became defensive when:

1. _____

_____

2. _____

_____

3. _____

_____

Three fights I need to relinquish, disengage myself from, in order to move on with my life:

1. _____

_____

2. _____

_____

3. _____

Three issues I flee from, which I need to stand up and engage:

1. _____

_____

2. _____

_____

3. _____

_____

For each fight I need to relinquish, I can take these practical steps to give up the fight:

1. _____

_____

2. _____

_____

3. _____

_____

For each issue that I need to engage, I can take these practical steps:

1. _____

2. _____

_____

3. _____

_____

"Do"—Get in the Mirror

Find a time in the bathroom or some other quiet place and take out a mirror. Spend a few minutes just standing and looking at you. What do you see about who you are? Ask yourself in what ways you are fighting others rather than fighting yourself. Be honest.

Pray this prayer: "God, reveal me to me. Show me who I am really fighting and who I am really fleeing."

Now make a list of characteristics, traits, and qualities that you wish you could change about yourself.

What I'd change about me   How I'm going to change it!

_____   _____

_____   _____

_____   _____

_____   _____

Now go back through your list and place a check next to the ones that you can directly improve upon through education, information, instruction, and practice—for instance, things like "better time management" or "work out regularly." Join a gym, get a book, take a class, and schedule the time to pursue those activities that will lead to your self-improvement.

Now consider the unchecked items that remain. They should be qualities that you think you cannot change or improve upon, things like "my quick temper" or "my need to be heard." Think through what it would mean to accept these qualities and no longer fight them. Having a quick temper can be a sign of intelligence, passion, and a strong sense of justice but may need to be balanced by patience and discipline. Instead of trying not to have a temper perhaps you should concentrate on choosing where to channel it—working out, fighting injustice, or serving others. Your need to be heard may come from a childhood where your ideas and opinions were ignored or belittled and as a result you never felt seen or acknowledged as a person. Instead of giving your opinion to anyone and everyone, why not consider volunteering with abused or neglected children or at a home for the elderly where people need someone to talk to? By giving them the attention you never got, you may go a long way to healing your own wounds.

Knowing which areas to change and which to accept can go a long way in helping you grow into a fighter who knows which battles to choose and which to let go.

eighteen

Knowing When to Walk Away and When to Stay

> *Before you begin this portion of the* Making Great Decisions Workbook, *read Chapter Eighteen, "Before You Take Flight" (pages 271–284), in* Making Great Decisions *(formerly titled* Before You Do).

Maturity necessitates that we know how to discern and decide when to roll up our sleeves and get down to the business of figuring out how to make something work. In our primary relationships, it can be too easy to run from the other person for innumerable reasons. Some people run when things are going too well; they're terrified to taste intimacy because they have been starving for it for so long that they fear it won't last. Other people don't want to face the hard work of loving someone when the going gets tough. These exercises will help you pick your battles and win them!

"Before" (Questions for Contemplation)

Follow the same process as in the previous chapters, with your pen handy.

1. When have you run away from a problem in your life? What did you learn about yourself in the midst of your flight? What was it you were really running from?

2. When have you stayed in a relationship that you should have left behind? What kept you in it as long as you did—what were you hoping would change?

3. How do you keep yourself from becoming cynical about love and romance? What or who helps you keep your hope alive?

4. Think about the people with whom you interact on a daily basis. How many of them are notably different from you? How often do you seek out similar people?

5. What will you do differently before you take flight from your next conflict or relational problem?

"You"

Review your affirmations from the previous chapter (page 179) and focus on any that you circled. Now, home in on your flight tendency, as emphasized in the revised affirmations below. Take quiet time again, for several consecutive days, to recite those you circled.

I am conscious of the areas in my life where I should be fighting more.

I am conscious of the past experiences that contributed to my inclination to avoid, to run.

I am conscious of what I am protecting myself from by running away from issues.

I am conscious that there is a present situation in my life that I have missed by fleeing.

I am often a peacemaker, but sometimes confrontation is necessary.

I have run away from some issues that need to be addressed.

I know what shaped this tendency in me.

I tend to pretend issues are not there or aren't problems.

With the present season of your life in mind, think about your tendency of letting go.

Identify one major area in your life where you have lingered too long. (Is there a familiar relationship that is no longer healthy or productive?)

_____

_____

_____

Identify three areas in your life where you have run.

_____

_____

_____

Identify three problems, issues, conflicts, or relationships from which you needed to take flight, but didn't, before the situation got much worse.

_____

_____

_____

Identify three problems, issues, conflicts, or relationships from which you ran, but which you might have stayed in successfully if *you'd known then what you know now about yourself.*

_____

_____

_____

"Do"

Make a list of what you know about yourself now that you did not know when you ran away from the situations you listed above.

_____

_____

_____

_____

_____

Your task this week is to choose one item from the list and write a strategy that would have been a step in improving that relationship or solving that problem, so you might not have had to run. In short, rewrite the script of one of those situations. Use this template to describe the situation:

The people involved were . . .

_____

_____

_____

What actually happened was . . .

_____

_____

_____

I ran from the situation by . . .

_____

_____

_____

Now that I know that I am . . .

_____

_____

_____

This is what I would have done . . .

_____

_____

_____

The following exercise is similar to one you did in the previous chapter on pages 180–187. Redo it now and see if your responses have changed.

Areas in my life where I presently need to be a peacemaker:

1. _____

_____

2. _____

_____

3. _____

_____

Areas in my life where I should be fighting more:

1. _____

_____

2. _____

_____

3. _____

_____

Past experiences that contributed to my inclination:

1. _____

_____

2. _____

_____

3. _____

_____

I am protecting myself from:

1. _____

_____

2. _____

_____

3. _____

_____

Present situations in my life that I have shunned:

1. _____

_____

2. _____

_____

3. _____

_____

Present situations in my life that I have attempted to fight:

1. _____

_____

2. _____

_____

3. _____

_____

I need to make peace with:

1. _____

_____

2. _____

_____

3. _____

_____

I have become weary and given up on these fights that I need to resume:

1. _____

_____

2. _____

_____

3. _____

_____

This tendency in me was shaped by:

1. _____

_____

2. _____

_____

3. _____

_____

I wrongly jumped to conclusions about:

1. _____

_____

2. _____

_____

3. _____

_____

I wrongly became suspicious about:

1. _____

_____

2. _____

_____

3. _____

_____

I wrongly became defensive when:

1. _____

_____

2. _____

_____

3. _____

_____

The fights I need to relinquish, disengage myself from, in order to move on with my life:

1. _____

_____

2. _____

_____

3. _____

_____

Three issues I flee from, which I need to stand up and engage:

1. _____

_____

2. _____

_____

3. _____

_____

For each fight I need to relinquish, I can take these practical steps to give up the fight:

1. _____

_____

2. _____

_____

3. _____

_____

For each issue I need to engage, I can take these practical steps:

1. _____

_____

2. _____

_____

3. _____

_____

Just as history repeats itself, so situations in our lives repeat themselves. List three ways you can conquer your urge to do any of the following listed actions and know when it is worth staying.

Avoiding	Fleeing	Taking off
Escaping	Letting go	Vanishing
Evading	Running away	Withdrawing

Ways I can conquer   It's worth it because . . .

_____   _____

_____   _____

_____   _____

nineteen

Making Smart Gambles

> *Before you begin this portion of the* Making Great Decisions Workbook, *read Chapter Nineteen, "Before You Gamble" (pages 285–294), in* Making Great Decisions *(formerly titled* Before You Do).

As we face new horizons and ventures, we can only be effective if we discern whether what we do is an investment in the future or a gamble in the moment. Here are strategies to help you know the difference.

"Before" (Questions for Contemplation)

Follow the same process as in the previous chapters, with your pen handy.

1. Do you enjoy gambling, such as playing cards, bingo, or the lottery? Where do you draw the line on how much you will gamble? How does this correlate to the way you take risks in life?

2. What regrets do you have about your past? What are the decisions you would change in order to recover the time lost to gambling rather than investing?

3. If someone interviewed those who know you, how would they describe your reputation? What is the present value of your name?

4. How are you investing the talents that God has given you? In what areas should you be taking more risks? Where have you risked too much?

5. In your experience, what is the difference between acting in faith and taking a gamble? What defines the difference between a leap of faith and a leap of folly?

"You"—Your Limits

Go back to your list of true values (page 6), which helped you clarify what is most important to you. Rewrite that list of the five things you value most, the things that are most important to you. (For example, being a good partner, being a reliable friend, keeping your word, always telling the truth, or being an excellent teacher, doctor, or father—whatever it is that you value most.)

_____   _____

_____   _____

_____   _____

_____   _____

Across from each item on your list, write what your reaction would be if you did something that caused you to lose it. Circle the things on the list that are your nonnegotiables—the things you cannot wager, that you cannot risk under any circumstances. These items set your gambling limits.

"Do"

Consider a present risk you are contemplating—going back to school, continuing a relationship, starting a new business, moving to a new job, or investing in a new corporate venture. Write out your answers to the following questions.

My primary motivation in taking this risk is:

_____

_____

_____

_____

My desired outcome is:

_____

_____

_____

_____

The results of my research and information gathering that inform my situation are:

_____

_____

_____

_____

I have discussed this with:

_____

_____

_____

_____

Their counsel was:

_____

_____

_____

I have spent time in prayer over this decision for (note how long, and which Scriptures you used):

_____

_____

_____

_____

After you've composed a few sentences answering each question, review them with a trusted friend or confidant before you make your final decision.

Summarize the key factors in the two columns below:

Risk of loss if decision turns out wrong

Consequences of letting it pass me by

_____   _____

_____   _____

_____   _____

_____   _____

_____   _____

_____   _____

_____   _____

Now go off on your own to your quiet place. Close your eyes. Sit quietly for a few minutes and pray.

Dear God,

    I have done all the work you asked me to.

    I've reflected and discerned; I've accepted responsibility; I've cleaned the junk from my trunk; I've decided who I want on my team; I've looked at where I join; I've researched, developed, and asked the twenty important questions; and more. I have placed my order for love, decided to risk, and resurrected my dreams. I've thought about my home, my children, my marriage, and what it would mean to divorce. I've decided what and what not to fight for. And now I step out and put my trust and faith in you.

    I ask to see not my will, but yours. And now that I've done the preparation, I ask that you lead and guide me in the direction you wish me to go. Amen.

And now you know what to do.

conclusion
Continue in the Way

Before you begin this portion of the Making Great Decisions Workbook, *read the Conclusion: Now You've Done It (pages 295–300), in* Making Great Decisions *(formerly titled* Before You Do*).*

This workbook has, I trust, whetted your appetite for a new process of making decisions, using solitude, journaling, affirmations, meditation, and prayer. You've finished the book, but I hope you will continue to make the practices you learned in this book a permanent part of your life. Make notebooks for writing down your thoughts—and reading them weeks, months, even years later—and pens fixtures in your life. Journaling can be a joy and a practical godsend. This workbook was your journal for the journey you've taken with me in reading *Making Great Decisions*. Now choose your own blank book and, as you spend quiet time in contemplation, recite your own affirmations, meditate, and pray. Fill the book's pages with the stuff of your triumphant life!